Ethnicity and Healthcare Practice

A guide for the primary care team

Ethnicity and Healthcare Practice

A guide for the primary care team

by

Lorraine Culley and Simon Dyson

QUAY
BOOKS

A division of MA Healthcare Ltd

Quay Books Division, MA Healthcare Ltd, St Jude's Church, Dulwich Road, London
SE24 0PB

British Library Cataloguing-in-Publication Data
A catalogue record is available for this book

© MA Healthcare Limited 2010
ISBN-10: 1-85642-366-2; ISBN-13: 978-1-85642-366-3

Printed by CLE, Huntingdon, Cambridgeshire

Contents

Introduction

There is a growing body of evidence to suggest that while minority ethnic groups experience the same range of illnesses as the UK population as a whole, many within such groups consistently report worse health than the general population. There is also evidence of increased prevalence of some specific conditions within some minority ethnic groups, such as higher rates of heart disease and diabetes within South Asian populations (Sproston and Nazroo, 2000).

The precise causes of ethnic differences in health status are less well-established, although a large amount of the ill health in minority ethnic groups can be explained by high levels of deprivation (Culley and Dyson, 2005). The groups with the worst health overall (the Pakistani and Bangladeshi communities) are those who experience the greatest degree of deprivation (Platt, 2002). The extensive work of James Nazroo and colleagues has established that social and economic inequalities, underpinned by racism, are the most significant fundamental causes of ethnic inequalities in health (Nazroo, 1997, 2001, 2003). Indeed the role of racism in ethnic health inequalities is of growing academic interest both in the USA and the UK (Karlsen, 2007). Close scrutiny of ethnicity data reveals big differences within minority groups in relation to both socio-economic status and gender. Risk factors (often the focal point for interventions) are the surface causes and intervening mechanisms of wider inequalities (Bhopal, 2007).

There is also evidence that the NHS, including primary care, has not always catered well to our multi-ethnic population and does not always offer healthcare which is easily accessible and culturally competent. The evidence base on service use and quality, however, is less well developed than that on ethnic differences in health per se. Nevertheless several studies have shown that some minority ethnic users report higher levels of dissatisfaction with NHS services, especially in primary care (Department of Health, 2008) and there are some examples of serious lapses in service provision (Aspinall and Jacobson, 2004).

The UK Government has a clear commitment to reduce health inequalities, although no specific national targets have been set with respect to minority ethnic groups. Despite a range of national and local initiatives (see Randhawa, 2007), it is difficult to assess the degree of progress in reducing health inequalities in the absence of robust evaluations of many interventions. This, of course, is made more difficult by the lack of reliable ethnicity data in the NHS, especially data from primary care. A recent Healthcare Commission report pointed out that there are no data on ethnicity for 90% of all contacts that patients have with their general practitioners (Healthcare Commission, 2009).

This book aims to provide a short overview of key issues in understanding the relationship between ethnicity and health, and to provide some practical suggestions and resources for primary healthcare providers in particular to consider when working with minority ethnic communities. A book of this size cannot aim to be comprehensive, but we make suggestions for further reading and include a list of useful resources to follow up the issues discussed and related topics.

Our aim is to shed some light onto the thorny issue of how ethnicity can be addressed within community healthcare practice. As we shall see, this involves more than identifying a list of ethnic 'groups' who allegedly share the same culture and behave in predetermined ways. Ethnicity and culture are likely to be just one set of structures (among others such as age, gender and sexuality) that many of us use in making sense of our lives generally and our understandings of health and illness. Culture may play an important role in showing how individuals and groups construct their identities. Our perceptions of health and illness, how we respond to the threat of illness and to treatment regimes are all potentially influenced by the taken-for-granted ideas of our culture as well as the medical/scientific knowledge we are able to draw on by our engagement with education, the media and the healthcare system (Kelleher, 1996). This is not to deny the significance of structures of inequality or the reality of racism, but to argue for an approach which extends our knowledge of how people draw upon elements of culture to help them manage the situations they face as patients or providers. In this respect, it is important to see ethnic identity not necessarily as a 'barrier' to good health, but also as a potentially positive source of support, which can contribute to the promotion of well-being. While it is undoubtedly the case that culture may influence health in many ways, we argue in this book that we should not view culture in a deterministic way, nor should we ignore the many similarities between ethnic groups in their experience of health and illness (Culley, 2006; Phillips, 2007).

Each chapter of the book includes a brief overview of a topic, examples of good practice/resources, a list of key points and suggestions for further reading.

We begin with an important discussion of key terms. There is much confusion in the medical and popular literature on just what we mean by 'race', 'ethnicity' and 'culture' and we begin by discussing these concepts in some detail. In *Chapter 2* we provide basic data on the ethnic composition of the UK population and discuss the importance of recognising the diversity within the minority ethnic population. The main religious and linguistic groups are described and we give examples of the ways in which health beliefs might impact on the encounter with primary care services. We argue that a cultural checklist approach is inappropriate. We provide a model for thinking about culture in the interaction between patient and provider. This is followed in *Chapter 3* by a discussion of managing diversity in healthcare practice. Here we cover important organisational issues such as ethnic data collection and ethnic monitoring and make some suggestions on taking a medical history. Important changes in the law on race equality and the implications for healthcare are also outlined.

The highly significant issue of communication support is tackled in *Chapter 4*. Language differences are widely perceived by both users and providers as presenting one of the main barriers to healthcare access and to delivering a high quality service to users. We give a breakdown of language diversity and some ideas for working with professional interpreters. The significance of linguistically and culturally appropriate health information is highlighted. Specific clinical areas are discussed in the *Chapter 5*. Minority ethnic populations broadly experience the same illnesses and conditions as the White population, but there is evidence that some conditions are also particularly prevalent among certain ethnic groups. Here we explore coronary heart disease, diabetes, hypertension, cancer, hepatitis and the haemoglobinopathies (sickle cell and thalassaemia) and discuss the potential impact of culture and religion on patient attitudes to medication.

Chapter 6 explores the management of illness in the context of family and community and the use of complementary or alternative therapies. In *Chapter 7* we focus on the issue of mental health and present evidence from large-scale community-based studies, some of which challenges data on mental health prevalence based on service use. We also explore the barriers to accessing mental health services and discuss the issue of substance misuse. The book concludes in *Chapter 8*, with a consideration of the challenges faced by asylum seekers and refugees in achieving good health and accessing healthcare in the UK.

The book is focused on the established minority ethnic communities in the UK, together with refugees and asylum seekers. At the present time, there is little information about the health status and health needs of the more recent 'economic' migrants from the new European states (EU8), although anecdotal evidence suggests that knowledge of services and language difficulties may well give rise to problems accessing services. For a review of these issues from a small-scale study in Scotland, see Orchard et al (2007).

References

Aspinall PJ, Jacobson B (2004) *Ethnic Disparities in Health and Health Care*. London: Department of Health.

Bhopal R (2007) *Ethnicity, Race and Health in Multicultural Societies*. Oxford University Press: Oxford

Culley L (2006) Transcending transculturalism? Race, ethnicity and healthcare. *Nursing Inquiry* **13**(2): 144–53.

Culley LA, Dyson SM (2005) 'Race' and Ethnicity. In Earle S, Denny E (eds) *An Introduction to the Sociology of Health: A Textbook for Nurses*. Polity Press, Cambridge

Department of Health (2008) *Report on Self-Reported Experiences of Patients from Black and Minority Ethnic Groups*. Department of Health, London

Healthcare Commission (2009) *Tackling the Challenge. Promoting Race Equality in the NHS in England*. Commission for Healthcare Audit and Inspection, London

Karlsen S (2007) *Ethnic Inequalities in Health: The impact of racism*. Race Equality Foundation Briefing Paper No.3. Race Equality Foundation, London

Kelleher D (1996) A defence of the use of the terms 'ethnicity' and 'culture'. In Kelleher D, Hillier S (eds) *Researching Cultural Differences in Health* (pp 69–90). Routledge, London

Orchard P et al (2007) *A Community Profile of EU8 Migrants in Edinburgh and an Evaluation of Their Access to Key Services*. Scottish Government Social Research. Available from: www.scotland.gov.uk/socialresearch

Nazroo JY (1997) *Ethnicity and Mental Health: Findings from a National Community Survey*. Policy Studies Institute, London

Nazroo JY (2001) *Ethnicity, Class and Health*. Policy Studies Institute, London

Nazroo J (2003) The structuring of ethnic inequalities in health: Economic position, racial discrimination and racism. *American Journal of Public Health* **93**(2): 277–84

Phillips A (2007) *Multiculturalism Without Culture*. Princeton University Press, Woodstock

Platt L (2002) *Parallel Lives? Poverty Among Ethnic Minority Groups in Britain*. Child Poverty Action Group, London

Randhawa G (2007) *Tackling Health Inequalities in Minority Ethnic Groups: Challenges and opportunities*. Race Equality Foundation Briefing Paper No.6. London: Race Equality Foundation

Sproston K, Nazroo J (eds) (2000) *Ethnic Minority Psychiatric Illness Rates in the Community (EMPIRIC) - Quantitative Report*. The Stationery Office, London

CHAPTER 1

Race, racism, ethnicity and culture

In this chapter we offer some explanation and definitions of key terms, such as race, ethnicity, racism, and racialisation, and question the traditional usage of ethnic categories as legitimate epidemiological variables in healthcare research and practice. We also introduce a way of thinking about culture and how it affects the provider–patient encounter.

The myth of distinct races

Scientific racism refers to a view of the world, promulgated by many in the scientific establishment of the 19th century, that humankind could be classified into distinct biological 'races'. Note that we put 'race' in inverted commas to indicate that we challenge the use of this term, and do not accept it at face value. Thus, in scientific racism, people were ascribed to 'races' such as 'Caucasian'. Not only were such 'races' distinct, but there was an implicit assumption that there was a hierarchy, with Caucasians allegedly superior to other 'races'. This type of thinking reached its high point with Nazi myths of the fitness of different 'races'. However, there are numerous authors (see *Box 1.1*) who have demonstrated the notion of distinct biological 'races' to be false. For example, Darwin (1871) rejects the idea of distinct races: '...it is hardly possible to discover clear distinctive characters between races because they "graduate into each other"'.

Box 1.1. Authors who have disputed the legitimacy of the term 'race'

Charles Darwin (1871) *The Descent of Man and Selection in Relation to Sex*
Ashley Montagu (1942) *Man's Most Dangerous Myth: The Fallacy of Race*
Steven Rose et al (1984) *Not in Our Genes*
Robert Miles (1993) *Racism After Race Relations*
Luigi Cavilli-Sforza et al (1996) *The History and Geography of Human Genes*
American Anthropological Association (1998) *Statement on 'Race'*
Bryan Sykes (2001) *The Seven Daughters Of Eve*

Moreover, 'Caucasian' refers to all European, Middle Eastern and Indian groups. However, if we look at the ABO blood system, identified by Hirszfeld and Hirszfeld (1919), we can see that the proportions of blood groups suggest a closer pattern between Africans and Europeans than between the allegedly equally 'Caucasian' European and Indian populations (see *Figure 1.1*).

Cavilli-Sforza et al (1996) propose three counter-arguments to the existence of 'races': genetic, geographic and statistical. First, genetic variation within populations is large compared to the amount of genetic variation between human populations. Second, all populations overlap when single genes are considered. In almost all populations all alleles are present but in different frequencies. Third, in historical terms, most polymorphisms ante-date the separation of humans into continents, this separation beginning when modern humans moved out of Africa 50000 years ago and replaced Neanderthal man.

Bryan Sykes (2001), the Oxford scientist who identified mitochondrial DNA passed down through the female line as the basis for tracing populations, cites the instance of two fishermen on a small island in the west of Scotland. One could assume that it is their geographic location that explains their genetic relationship. They are indeed related, but through genetic ancestries that circumnavigated the world in opposite directions:

These stories, and others like them, make a nonsense of any biological basis for racial classifications.

Sykes (2001: 295)

However, the notion of 'races' has much wider resonance, not least because major institutions have not yet developed the terminology to deal

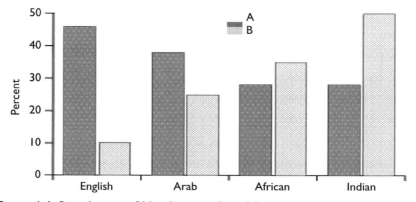

Figure 1.1: Distribution of blood groups A and B among major populations. Adapted from Cavalli-Sforza et al (1996: 18).

with these complex issues. Thus, from the 1960s onwards, UK policy has referred to 'race relations'. The problem is that if there are no 'races', it makes little sense to refer to relations between them. However, in the UK, the term 'race' has inadvertently been given official legitimacy because it has been used in the title of legislation, such as the Race Relations (Amendment) Act 2000, and in the title of official bodies designed to monitor and challenge discrimination, such as the former Commission for Racial Equality. When arguably progressive legislation and official bodies are themselves constructed around the idea of 'race', it then becomes very difficult to move beyond this false concept (Culley and Demaine, 2006).

Sociologists have increasingly encouraged use of the term 'ethnicity', However, ethnicity is frequently confused with other terms, such as nationality or country of birth.

Nationality is the nation state of which you have citizenship. Since the 1981 British Nationality Act became law in January 1983, being born on British soil does not automatically confer British citizenship onto a person.

Country of birth is your place of birth and it is not the same thing as ethnicity.

Ethnicity refers to people who share a family lineage and an association with an identifiable geographic territory. They may (although not necessarily) also share one or more of such factors as religion, language, dress, diet, and customs. Ethnicity is something we all have. We all have an ancestry, links to one or more territories, and a range of social customs around birth, marriage and death. To talk about 'ethnic diet', 'ethnic dress' or 'my ethnic clients' is therefore to be referring to *all* diets, *all* dress codes and *all* clients. When people do mistakenly use these phrases they usually mean 'people who are different from me'. Ethnic minority usually means an ethnic group that is in the minority numerically speaking, and usually that it is less powerful economically or politically than the ethnic majority groups. However in some areas, for example South Africa or Guatemala, the numerical majority is the economically less powerful, therefore the two aspects of 'minority' do not necessarily coincide. Furthermore, the term 'minority' positions certain peoples in ways they may find oppressive and offensive:

The term 'minority' has connotations of 'less important' or 'marginal'. In many settings it is not only insulting but also mathematically misleading or inaccurate. Further, its use perpetuates the myth of white homogeneity – the notion that everyone who does not belong to a minority is by that token a member of a majority in which there are no significant differences or tensions.

Parekh (2000: xxiii)

However, since the terminology on ethnicity continues to be the subject of much dispute, and we have to find one way of referring to complex issues, we have chosen to refer in this book to minority ethnic peoples, with the minority usually referring both to being relatively less powerful, and to being in the numerical minority within those people resident in the UK.

Racialisation

This term refers to a process whereby a status, including health status, caused by social, political, economic or historically specific circumstances is falsely attributed to an ethnic group on the basis of presumed biological or cultural characteristics. Consider the work of the statistician Sir Karl Pearson in the 19th century. Pearson wanted to 'prove' the lack of genetic fitness of the Jewish race. However, if one were to look at the impoverished Jewish immigrants to Britain in the latter half of the 19th century one would expect to see people smaller in stature because of an impoverished diet, and generally unhealthy because of the diseases associated with poverty, poor housing, and exposure to dangerous employment, including such diseases as tuberculosis, vitamin deficiencies, infections and so forth. Pearson developed his statistical test, the Pearson product-moment correlation (Pearson's r) to 'demonstrate' the link between Jews and poor health.

However, correlation (or statistical association) is not causation. The superficial link between membership of the Jewish ethnic group and ill-health was simply a by-product of an entirely understandable link between poverty and ill-health. However, in attributing this link to an inherent cultural or genetic inferiority of the Jewish race, Pearson was guilty of racialisation: giving a false sense of naturalness and concreteness to an association born of specific social, economic and historical circumstances.

Nor is this racialisation a historical phenomenon. Nazroo (1999) has argued that this process of racialisation lies behind the mistaken concept of 'Asian' heart disease. In fact, when different levels of material deprivation in ethnic groups of people of Indian, Pakistani and Bangladeshi descent are taken into account, most of the differences in reported levels of heart health between these 'Asian' groups and 'White' groups disappear. Another potential example of racialisation is the notion that Asian babies are smaller. However, we need to consider if this is merely a consequence of the lower standard of living of South Asian migrants in the 1960s and 1970s as they entered low paid dangerous work in the textile industries and elsewhere. Furthermore, whenever waves of migration occur to take up low paid jobs in the UK, then those migrant groups will very likely exhibit compromised health states compared to the more affluent host communities. Again, it would be very easy to look at the new migrants of the future and come to the (erroneous) conclusion that their relative poor health is attributable to either their genetic make-up or to their cultural health behaviours. Nor is it necessarily the case that this relationship will always be in the same direction. The Government's highly skilled migrant worker status (even with its recent and more restrictive replacement, the so-called 'Tier One' category of a new points-based immigration system) available to attract migrants qualified in shortage areas of the professional and technical labour force, could mean that certain sections of migrants, entering professional jobs, could experience relatively better health outcomes because of raised socio-economic status. However, another possibility here is that discrimination would keep well-qualified personnel at socio-economic levels below their potential and actually obscure the relationship between levels of material deprivation and health status. Two recent comprehensive reviews of ethnic health inequalities have shown clearly that for each apparent 'difference' between the majority population and a minority ethnic group, there are significant differences within minority groups, suggesting that simple genetic or cultural explanations for ill health are unlikely to be correct (Aspinall and Jacobson, 2004).

Culture

In the UK, early health service attempts to come to grips with 'culture' ended up blaming those cultures for ill-health. This was because such attempts emphasised 'unusual' practices which were then viewed as deviant from the allegedly healthy 'norms' of the ethnic majority. Some examples of such ethnocentric health campaigns are given in *Box 1.2*.

First, in trying to explain health behaviours by reference to different 'cultures', we end up by ignoring the diversity that exists within cultures that are supposedly homogenous. The notion of a 'Black Caribbean' identity, for instance, is a product of the historical circumstances in which people of disparate and diverse islands and parts of the South American mainland hundreds of miles apart come to be in Britain. This means that, for example, some people of Caribbean birth could well be of Indian, Chinese and Irish, as well as African descent.

Second, the emphasis on cultural difference ignores the extent of similarities between different ethnic groups. For example, the US sociologist Eliot Freidson (1970) developed the concept of the 'lay referral network' to express the idea that, before formally becoming patients, those who are ill may check out their symptoms with others, such as family, friends, or work colleagues, in order to assess whether or not they should go to see their doctor. They may also self-medicate, seek 'alternative' treatments, or refer to a respected religious figure, such as a local priest. It would be possible to examine the health-seeking behaviour of, say, British Pakistani Muslims and to find that they seek advice from a mother-in-law, from an alternative healer such as a hakim, or from an imam (priest). Taken in isolation it would be possible to misrepresent the health behaviours of British Pakistani Muslims as different or as 'part of their culture'. However, these patterns may also be present in other ethnic groups.

Cultures are not static but are continually changing and evolving. Cultural identity is historically and socially situated. Sometimes the culture is itself partially formed around opposition to a perceived hostility, either local or geopolitical. For example, Sikhism coalesced into a stronger identity following campaigns around the use of the turban and motor-cycle crash helmets in the UK, and around the reaction to the 1984 storming of the holiest Sikh shrine, the Golden Temple in Amritsar. Islam in the UK has forged a particular identity since the war in Iraq.

There are many factors other than ethnicity that contribute to a culture. Culture is equally derived from gender, level of income, generation and other power relations as much as ethnicity to which it is too often reduced

---

Box 1.2. Examples of ethnocentric health campaigns

- **Asian Mother and Baby Campaign:** This campaign did not take account of levels of material deprivation. It assumed the problem was to coach undifferentiated Asian mothers to use services correctly. It placed South Asian link-workers in the invidious position of being employed to advocate against their employer on behalf of the mothers (Rocheron, 1988)
- **Stop Rickets Campaign:** This campaign assumed the problem was one of culture – insufficient exposure to the sun (because of Asian clothes or not going out of doors) or poor Asian diet. Did not take account of levels of material deprivation, nor of the role, for the ethnic majority, of fortifying basic foodstuffs like margarine with Vitamin D (Ahmad, 1996)
- **Surma:** A campaign from the 1970s against the cultures that used traditional eye cosmetics, some of which were lead-based. The campaign ignored plausible environmental sources of lead in inner-city housing areas (from local industry, petrol, lead pipes, lead paint, etc) and the fact that not all such preparations contained lead. Health education leaflets were translated into Asian languages for this issue decades before leaflets addressing numerically more significant issues, such as heart disease, hypertension, diabetes, strokes or mental health were produced (Pearson, 1986)
- **Consanguinity:** Studies were based on poorly defined concepts of consanguinity and/or ethnicity and poorly controlled for levels of material deprivation. It was mistakenly assumed that all Pakistani Muslim marriages were consanguineous (Ahmad, 1994; Darr, 2009)

(Ahmad, 1996). In an early example of this, Ahmad et al (1989) found that the supposedly 'cultural' preference of Asian women for a female GP was, on closer examination, a preference for a GP who spoke a relevant language.

Finally, culture may be a source of nurturing and strength (Ahmad, 1996). Thus, for example, it has been suggested that concentration of some minority ethnic groups in certain residential areas may have positive health effects through community integration and social support, which may even offset any health damage from the poor material environment often found in the urban areas where minority ethnic groups predominantly live. Furthermore, it is conceivable that high levels of unemployment may enable people to undertake extensive lay caring roles, and that an otherwise positive social development in ending high unemployment rates may break down a hidden lay network of caring only made possible by that unemployment (Mir, 2005).

How people respond to and live within a particular culture will vary according to their socio-economic status, their gender and their age. Think

---

Box 1.3. Examples of flexible culture

- **Eating habits**: Do all Christians eat fish on a Friday? Do all White British people drink tea? Some will drink tea, and sometimes in a symbolic way that signals more than refreshment, as in 'tea and sympathy'. However, others may not drink tea because they prefer coffee. Some will not drink tea or coffee because they do not drink anything with caffeine in it because they regard it as a drug and some believe it may prompt a migraine.

- **Church-going**: Some may only go to church on special occasions such as christenings and weddings, or perhaps at special times of year, such as carol services at Christmas, or perhaps at times of family crisis to pray for the health of a loved one who is ill. There are many who regard themselves as believing in the Christian God, but who never go to church or express their beliefs formally.

- **Alcohol**: Some may not drink alcohol and may not like the atmosphere and culture of pubs, but may go there because it is the major venue for meeting their friends.

- **Healthcare**: It could be said that the manner in which health professionals are expected to respond to death, pain and distress in clients and relatives has changed over the generations, from a cold, detached 'stiff upper lip' to one of greater emotional expression. Being ill, or being in hospital may itself change what people want: someone may change their eating and drinking habits because they want to 'cheer themselves up' or 'treat themselves' because they are ill or in unfamiliar surroundings. An illness may make people intolerant of foods they would otherwise wish to have.

about disaggregating the idea of homogenous ethnic groups. There are significant differences within both 'White' and minority ethnic groups. We all need our ethnic identity to be respected, but we cannot be understood just in terms of our ethnicity. We also need to bear in mind that culture is constantly changing and evolving and is not a fixed property of individuals (see *Box 1.3*). We do behave according to cultural norms (what we eat, how we interact, etc) but they are flexible guidelines rather than rules that rigidly determine our behaviour. Thinking about culture in this way could help to avoid stereotyping patients.

Key points

- It is not accurate to think in terms of distinct biological races.
- We need to distinguish between the distinct categories of nationality, country of birth and ethnicity.
- 'Racialisation' is the process of falsely attributing observed differences in health to presumed genetic or cultural characteristics, rather than to historically specific social and economic circumstances.
- Cultures are diverse and changeable over time and between settings.
- Cultural characteristics are flexible guidelines for living rather than prescriptive rules.

References

Ahmad W (1996) The trouble with culture. In: Kelleher D, Hillier S eds. *Researching Cultural Differences in Health*. Routledge, London: 190–219

Ahmad W, Kernohan E, Baker M (1989) Patients' choice of general practitioner: Influence of patients' fluency in English and the ethnicity and sex of the doctor. *Journal of the Royal College of General Practitioners* **39**: 153–5

American Anthropological Association (1998) *Statement on 'Race'*. Available at: http://www.aaanet.org/stmts/racepp.htm [accessed 25th Sept 2007]

Aspinall PJ, Jacobson B (2004) *Ethnic Disparities in Health and Health Care*. London: Department of Health

Cavilli-Sforza LL, Menozzi P, Piazza A (1996) *The History and Geography of Human Genes*. Abridged edn, Princeton University Press, Princeton, NJ

Culley L, Demaine J (2006) Ethnic Ideologies and Public Policy. In E Rata, R Openshaw (eds) *Public Policy and Ethnicity: The Politics of Ethnic Boundary-Making* Basingstoke, Palgrave Macmillan

Darr A (2009) Cousin marriage, culture blaming and equity in service delivery. *Diversity in Health and Care* **6**(1): 7–9

Darwin C (2004 [1871]) *The Descent of Man and Selection in Relation to Sex*. Penguin, London

Freidson E (1970) *Profession of Medicine*. Dodd, Mead and Company, New York

Hirszfeld L, Hirszfeld H (1919) Essai d'application des méthodes au problème des races *Anthropologie* **29**: 505–37.

Miles R (1993) *Racism After Race Relations*. Routledge, London

Mir G (2005) *Social Policy and Health Inequalities:The relevance of faith to chronic illness management in the Pakistani community*. PhD University of Leeds Medical School

Montagu A (1998) *Man's Most Dangerous Myth: The Fallacy of Race* 6th edn. Alta Mira Press, Walnut Creek, CA. Originally published 1942

Nazroo JY (1999) The racialization of inequalities in health. In: Dorling D, Simpson S eds. *Statistics in Society: The Arithmetic of Politics*. Arnold, London: 215–22

Parekh B (2000) *The Future of Multi-Ethnic Britain*. London: Runneymede Trust

Rocheron Y (1988) The Asian Mother and Baby Campaign: The construction of the ethnic minorities' health needs. *Critical Social Policy* (22): 4–23

Rose S, Lewontin R, Kamin L (1984) *Not in our Genes: Biology, Ideology and Human Nature*. Harmondsworth: Penguin

Sykes B (2001) *The Seven Daughters of Eve*. Bantam Press, London

Further reading

Ahmad W (1994) Reflections on the consanguinity and birth outcome debate. *Journal of Public Health Medicine* **16**(4): 423–8

Aspinall PJ (2001) Operationalising the collection of ethnicity data in studies of the sociology of health and illness. *Sociology of Health and Illness* **23**(6): 829–62

Bhopal RS (2007) Ethnicity, race and health in multicultural societies. Oxford: Oxford University Press. Chapters 1–3: 1–90

Kelleher D (1996) A defence of the use of the terms 'ethnicity' and 'culture'. In: Kelleher D, Hillier S eds. *Researching Cultural Differences in Health*. Routledge, London: 69–90

Pearson M (1986) Racist notions of ethnicity and culture in health education. In: Rodmell S, Watt A eds. *The Politics of Health Education*. Routledge and Kegan Paul, London

CHAPTER 2

Ethnic groups in the UK

In this chapter, we provide a numerical description of the main ethnic groups in the UK, in terms of country of birth, ethnic group, religious group and languages spoken. However, we do not attempt to assign a list of basic traditions to each group, but rather to use the diversity of groups in the UK to help the health professional identify domains of patient experience, by which is meant such areas of living as diet, rites and washing, around which there may be differences of importance to the patient, and which may affect the delivery of healthcare. However, we do not suggest that these are differences that can be automatically 'read-off' from being ascribed membership of an ethnic group.

The main countries of birth of residents in the UK

In the UK Census, 2001, about 7.5% of the UK population was born abroad. *Table 2.1* lists the countries in which migrants were born in descending order.

There are a number of factors to bear in mind when reflecting on communities who have migrated to the UK. Populations are affected by emigration, as well as immigration, and the UK is no exception. For example, between 1975 and 2001, 50 000 immigrants from the Indian Sub-continent and 25 000 from the Caribbean emigrated from the UK (Rendall and Ball, 2004). Substantial numbers of people are born abroad in both the Republic of Ireland and in what have come to be known as Old Commonwealth countries, such as Australia, New Zealand and Canada. A substantial proportion of immigrants to the UK are White, Christian and English-speaking, quite contrary to the impression given by the headlines in more sensationalist newspapers.

Patterns of settlement are unlikely to be evenly spread across the country. 'Chain migration' refers to the phenomenon in which early settlers gave a focus for later settlers, providing a measure of security, orientation, and shared resources. This makes settlement easier for the later arrivals. Although much migration historically has been, and will likely continue to be, migration undertaken in order to take up lower paid and dangerous occupations not attractive to others, there is also the Government's Tier One of the points-based immigration system, which, although more restrictive than the highly skilled migrant worker status, still suggests that a proportion

Table 2.1. British residents born abroad (UK Census, 2001)

Republic of Ireland	494 850	Turkey	53 964
India	466 416	China	51 717
Pakistan	320 767	Zimbabwe	49 303
Germany	262 276	Malaysia	49 207
Other South and		Former Yugoslavia	47 410
East Africa	196 651	Somalia	43 515
USA	155 030	Former USSR	43 182
Bangladesh	154 201	Iran	42 377
South Africa	140 201	Singapore	40 180
Kenya	129 356	Netherlands	39 972
Other Far East	118 704	Japan	37 293
Italy	107 002	Portugal	36 402
Australia	106 404	Greece	35 007
Hong Kong	94 611	Iraq	32 251
France	94 611	Sweden	22 366
Nigeria	88 105	Belgium	21 498
Other Central and		Austria	19 511
West Africa	86 444	Denmark	18 493
Cyprus	77 156	Sierra Leone	16 972
South America	76 412	Afghanistan	14 890
North Africa	71 923	Czech Republic	12 077
Other Middle East	71 635	Finland	11 228
Canada	70 145	Democratic Republic	
Sri Lanka	67 832	of Congo	8590
Poland	60 680	Romania	7617
New Zealand	57 916	Albania	2270
Spain	54 105	Luxembourg	1236

From: Born Abroad http://news.bbc.co.uk/1/shared/spl/hi/uk/05/born_abroad/html/ overview.stm [accessed 1 June 2009].

of migrants will have professional backgrounds. As discussed previously, country of birth does not necessarily tell us about a person's ethnicity. For example, those born in East or South Africa and now resident in the UK could be of White, Indian or Black African descent.

Migration has been a defining feature of the British experience for over 2000 years: one recent migration brought nearly half a million Polish people to the UK and this is just one example of this regular feature. More recently there has been a substantial return migration to Poland. This immigration and emigration is ironically a product of the free movement of labour within the European Union. Restrictive immigration policies (such as the 1962 Commonwealth Immigrants Act) deterred return migration to the Caribbean, for example, because migrants were effectively placed in the position of having to make a once-and-for-all decision.

The main ethnic groups in the UK

The UK Census of 2001 was only the second census to collect data on ethnic origins and was the first to collect data on religion. In collecting data on ethnicity, as opposed to country of birth, for example, the UK stands outside the experience of most of the rest of Europe. In 2001 nearly 8% of the UK population was from a minority ethnic group (12% of population of England and Wales). Recent estimates from the Office for National Statistics (ONS) suggest that this had grown to around 11% in 2006 (Healthcare Commission 2009). The fastest growing group is the Chinese population, followed by Black African and Asian groups. The Black Caribbean group show the lowest increase since 2001. Experimental population estimates by ethnic group

Table 2.2. The main ethnic groups in the UK in 2001			
Ethnic group	Total population	% of total population	% of minority ethnic population
White	54 153 898	92.1	n/a
Mixed	677 117	1.2	14.6
Asian or Asian British			
Indian	105 3411	1.8	22.7
Pakistani	747 285	1.3	16.1
Bangladeshi	283 063	0.5	6.1
Other Asian	247 664	0.4	5.3
Black or Black British			
Black Caribbean	565 876	1.0	12.2
Black African	485 277	0.8	10.5
Black Other	97 585	0.2	2.1
Chinese	247 403	0.4	5.3
Other	230 615	0.4	5.0
All minority ethnic populations	4 635 296	7.9	100.0
All populations	58 789 194	100.0	

From: UK Census, April 2001, Office for National Statistics. National Statistics (www. statistics.gov.uk)

Crown copyright material is reproduced with the permission of the Controller of HMSO

(2001–2007) are now available for each Primary Care Trust and Strategic Health Authority on the ONS website (www.statistics.gov.uk). *Table 2.2* shows the main responses to the ethnicity question in the UK 2001 Census.

Once again, there are several important caveats in terms of working with these figures. The categories are bureaucratic pseudo-legalistic creations, developed (albeit on the basis of past experience, testing of pilot categories by the Office for National Statistics, and consultations with minority ethnic communities themselves) for the purpose of compiling State statistics. This means that there are no naturally occurring real people who unambiguously correspond to these categories. This is easier to think about if one realises that the categories themselves have changed since the 1991 Census. It becomes harder to remember these are artificial creations because the Department of Health has instructed that ethnic data within the health services should be collected in terms of these categories.

Second, the category 'White' conceals a great deal of ethnic diversity. The term is sometimes misleadingly used as if it were co-terminous with the concept of the 'ethnic majority', a majority both in the numerical and the power sense of that term. But the category includes a number of groups who themselves experience racism, including those of Jewish, Irish, Southern European, East European and Arab descent. In the case of the Irish, there is evidence to suggest that, overall, this group suffers compromised health status and receives a poor level of health service, even compared to other minority groups. Furthermore, their relative health also depends upon whether we mean those from Eire or Northern Ireland, those of Protestant or Catholic faith, and those who are first generation or subsequent generation migrants to Britain (Greenslade et al, 1997).

Third, there is now a sizeable proportion of the population who consider themselves of mixed ethnicity, even when they are given a very restricted set of 'combinations' (White/Black; White/Asian or White/Other) from which to choose. This will present an increasing challenge to any health services organised around 'reading-off' needs from ethnic categories. This is because it will not be clear that someone of so-called 'mixed' ethnicity will identify with the traditions of their mother, their father, a position somewhere between the two, or will develop a completely new cultural position. The possibilities for flexibility and change in culture are perhaps more readily identified in those of 'mixed' ethnicities, but there is no reason why the same flexibilities and changing identities are not also open to those who tick a single bureaucratic category in any ethnic question.

Both the Asian British and the Black British categories contain within them a great deal of diversity, a diversity not reflected in references to 'Black' or 'Asian' clients. The following are examples of sources of diversity within ethnic groups.

- *Gender*: Partly as a result of discrimination in the labour market against black males, Black Caribbean females have a comparatively high rate of participation in the paid labour market.
- *Migrant/British-born*: Caribbean-born migrants who entered nursing in the 1950s and 1960s were more tolerant both of poor working conditions in nursing and of racism than the hosts had any right to expect. Their children and grandchildren are more likely to challenge racism directly, and may shun nursing as a career on the basis of the way their elders were treated within the NHS, creating a challenge to recruiting for diversity today.
- *Reason for migration*: Reasons include forced economic migration, forced political migration (refugee), and forced political migration (individual political persecution, asylum seeker). Other reasons include voluntary economic migration to low paid or professional/technical job (highly skilled migrant status) or to maintain family networks (including marriage). Migration may be legally sanctioned or illegal.
- *Age and generation:* Population age structures of minority ethnic groups are generally younger than the 'White' ethnic category. This may mean their health needs are disproportionately higher or lower for certain age groups. Younger age structures will mean numerically greater needs in terms of maternal and child health, but less in terms of the health of older people. However, the latter may mean that very few effective services have been developed in the areas of care of elders or palliative care, for example.
- *Housing*: Quality of housing is generally inversely related to health status. However, otherwise less desirable housing in terms of environmental quality may be off-set by the benefits of living within reach of social support networks, public spaces where they feel physically safe and culturally relevant shops and services.
- *Language*: British Asians (Pakistani) may speak English, Urdu, Punjabi or Pashto. British Asians (Indian) may speak English, Gujarati, Hindi, Punjabi, or Kutchi. British Asians (Bangladeshi) may speak English, Bengali or Sylheti.
- *Religion*: British Asians (Indian) may be Hindu, Sikh, Jain or Muslim, amongst other religions
- *Racism*: Black African and Black Caribbeans experience racism on the basis of their skin colour. British Muslims experience racism on the basis of their culture and religion.
- *Socio-economic status*: Brought from India and occupying an intermediate position between the White British colonists and the local African population, East African Asians developed business skills. Although downwardly mobile upon forced migration to Britain in the

1960s and 1970s, this group has been the most economically upwardly mobile migrant group over the past 40 years. This is reflected in their reported heart health being as good as, if not better than, the 'White' ethnic group.

- *Health services*: With the exception of Chinese and White Irish, minority ethnic groups in the UK consult with GPs in proportion to their health statuses. However, they are less likely to be referred to hospital specialisms.
- *Life history*: Someone who has fled violence, torture or rape in their homeland may experience a physical medical examination, or a routine procedure such as a bed bath, in the light of their life history experience.

The main religious groups in the UK

Unlike the 1991 Census, the 2001 Census contained a question on religion, although answering this question was optional. *Table 2.3* shows the approximate distributions of religious faiths within each of the 2001 UK Census ethnic categories.

Although the UK is diverse in both ethnic and religious terms, the overwhelming majority of the population (around 7 in 10) describe themselves as both White and Christian. Around 15% of the population stated that they had no religion. The Indian ethnic groups were perhaps the

Table: 2.3. Percentages of reported religious affiliations of different ethnic groups in the UK in 2001

	Christian	Hindu	Muslim	Sikh	Other religion	No religion /not stated
White	75				1	24
Mixed	52		10		3	35
Indian		45	13	29		6
Pakistani	1		92			7
Bangladeshi	1		92			7
Black African	68		22			10
Black Caribbean	74				1	25
Chinese	22				15	63

Source: Adapted from Office for National Statistics: UK Census, April 2001
National Statistics website: www.statistics.gov.uk
Crown copyright material is reproduced with the permission of the Controller of HMSO

Table 2.4. The largest ethnic/faith groups in UK 2001	
	Numbers
White Christians	36 000 000
White No Religion	750 000
Black African and Black Caribbean Christians	810 000
Pakistani Muslims	658 000
Indian Hindus	467 000
Mixed ethnicity Christians	347 000
Indian Sikhs	301 000
Bangladeshi Muslims	260 000
White Jews	252 000

Source: Adapted from Office for National Statistics: UK Census, April 2001
National Statistics website: www.statistics.gov.uk
Crown copyright material is reproduced with the permission of the Controller of HMSO

most diverse in religious terms with 45% describing themselves as Hindu, 29% as Sikh and 13% as Muslim. The most homogenous groups, by contrast, were those of Pakistani and Bangladeshi descent of whom over 90% said they were Muslims.

By far the largest group numerically are those who self-ascribe to the categories 'White' and 'Christian' (*Table 2.4*). The next largest group are those who subscribe to no religion at all, including over seven million of those who ticked the ethnic category 'White'. Self-designation as having no religion applied to half the Chinese population and a quarter of those with 'mixed' ethnicity. By contrast those of Black African, Indian, Pakistani, Bangladeshi, and White Irish were all groups in which very few claimed to have no religion. Some ethnic and religious groups are nearly co-terminous. For instance, nearly all (97%) of those who recorded themselves as Jewish placed themselves in the 'White' category in terms of their ethnicity. Likewise an overwhelming majority (91%) of those of the Sikh faith also selected the ethnicity category British Asian (Indian).

The main linguistic groups in the UK

At the time of writing, there is no official source giving a detailed breakdown of how many people in the UK have English as a second language. Indeed a question about languages spoken was not asked in the 2001 Census, although pressure is growing for it to be included in the 2011 Census. However, Census information leaflets and questions were translated into the 25 languages, listed in *Table 2.5*.

Table 2.5. Main languages used for 2001 Census material		
Albanian/Kosovan	Greek	Serbian
Arabic	Gujarati	Somali
Bengali	Hindi	Spanish
Cantonese	Italian	Swahili
Croatian	Japanese	Turkish
Farsi/Persian	Polish	Urdu
English	Portuguese	Vietnamese
French	Punjabi	Welsh
German	Russian	

The issues raised in providing a service for those whose first language is not English are discussed in *Chapter 4*.

Domains of interest

One of the areas that health professionals frequently request further training in is 'cultural awareness'. What is usually meant by this phrase is that the person concerned is looking for a list of ethnic groups and their corresponding cultural rules and rituals about food, religious festivals and observances, washing, dress, and other customs that might 'get in the way' of conventional healthcare practices. However, as we have already seen in *Chapter 1*, culture is far more flexible and a person's health needs are a complex product of gender, age, and status, as well as ethnicity, and individual life history, and cannot easily be 'read-off' from their ethnicity. This leaves the health professional with a dilemma. One could try to learn the principles of a number of cultures and religions and respond to a patient's presumed needs on this basis. However, this does not meet the flexibility of culture and may indeed lead to harmful stereotyping. On the other hand, one could revert back to the position of treating everyone as an individual. This is arguably a position which has a superficial attractiveness as being somehow intuitively 'fair' or 'equal' and indeed of attending to individual patient need. However, this depends on the health professional being fully aware of what areas of life even potentially comprise domains around which there may be important cultural differences.

For example, for a number of religions, including Islam and Sikhism, not cutting hair has an important significance. This means that loss of hair through medical procedures (shaving for operations), medical treatments (hair loss associated with some cancer treatments), or medical conditions (alopecia) will represent a challenge for some patients. However, (and this is where some naïve views of multiculturalism have misled practitioners in the past) it seems to us that the potential cultural significance of body hair is a domain of experience around which practitioners may reasonably anticipate some variation in patient preferences. To treat all patients equally will not work because, while we can readily anticipate some domains of experience that may be culturally influenced (such as food preferences) we may not even realise that some issues (such as rituals of washing) represent a cultural domain of experience at all, and therefore not realise the attendant possibility of important cultural variation in beliefs around that domain.

Thus, while we do not advocate health professionals starting to 'learn' cultures in a programmatic way so that these cultural sensitivities can be applied to patients who 'belong' to that culture, neither can we endorse an approach that is only based on individual patients. Instead what we wish to propose is that, through a combination of formal education, self-directed learning and experience, health professionals widen their knowledge about cultural practices. This does not mean primarily 'learning' these practices by rote. Rather it means that the experience of having one's mindset about the world challenged, widened, or reformulated can help develop a more 'open' thinking that is more attuned to possible variations in patient preferences and obligations, variations that may as yet be unknown to the health professional. Once these domains are identified in the health professional's mind, all patients may be asked how the proposed treatment may affect them, and negotiating the course of action with the patient can then begin.

Food

One of the more obvious domains around which there are patient differences is the area of food choices.

According to Gunaratnam (2001), there are several influences on patient behaviour.

- A preference (for vegetarian food) that cuts across ethnic or religious divides.
- A liking for a food outside of one's own tradition (perhaps, psychologically as a 'treat' to mark special circumstances or as a way of cheering oneself up in adversity).
- A recognition that the illness itself means that previously preferred foods can not now be tolerated.
- A rejection of a short-cut version of food preparation, not based on raw ingredients.
- A view that institutional food was poor and that an institution could never provide food choices matched to individual need.

Again note that each of these responses to food could equally well be given by a White British Christian patient as well. To this extent, to regard these responses as somehow denoting a distinct culture would be to over-emphasise the differences between different ethnic groups. According to Gunaratnam (2001: 175–6) naïve multi-culturalism also denies choice to White English patients:

> … *a nursing auxiliary, in a discussion about caring, observed, 'We've got a chap on the ward at the moment, he's English and his Gran brings him in pie and mash. He loves pie and mash, and maybe three times week he has his pie and mash… or pie and liquor.'*
> *What this example illustrates is a common omission within multi-culturalism, that is, how cultural experiences of Englishness also have implications for service provision. In broad terms, the choices of many White, English people are also not met by services and some of these choices may relate to cultural experiences of age, class and region. For both English and non-English service users then, there are practical limitations in providing for a diversity of choices. However, through the association of multi-culturalism with 'exotic' differences largely based upon differences of colour, ethnicity, culture and religion, the experiences of non-White people can become marginalised, not simply through processes of exclusion but also through more subtle processes of inclusion. At the same time, the experiences of the ethnic majority are seen to fall outside the concerns of multi-culturalism, so that experiences of 'Whiteness' or 'Englishness' are seen as unproblematic and one-dimensional.*

This is a form of service provision in which all the main different ethnic groups in the locality are accorded one identifying characteristic of each domain of their culture, in this case food choices. The health service menu might have one 'White', one 'Asian' and one vegetarian choice.

Trying to read-off needs from ethnic categories fails in a number of ways for the Pakistani and Bangladeshi clients.

> *A Pakistani woman, a lone parent, without relatives in this country, said that when in the hospice she chose the vegetarian option because she rarely ate meat and also liked to have English food. In another case, a carer told me that her husband, who was Pakistani, had chosen the Kosher food because he could not tolerate spicy food at that stage of his illness, although she also added that she felt he did not like the halal food, speculating that it was probably cooked using curry paste and not raw spices. A Bangladeshi man told me that his wife or brother-in-law always*

brought him home-cooked food, because the halal food in the hospice was 'completely bad'. In common with other service users, he doubted that the hospice could ever provide him with food that could meet his individual preferences.

Gunaratnam (2001:175)

But Gunaratnam points out that such an approach also fails the 'White English' client because it ignores the dimensions of regional, generational and social class preferences. By superficially including Asian clients in such a scheme, the dimensions of region, generation, and perhaps of caste, sect, or tradition, important to their experience are downplayed or ignored, as much as they are for the White patient.

Religious observances

One of the main stereotypes sometimes imputed to those who hold religious beliefs in a secular society is that those who maintain faith are inevitably ignorant of medical science and/or fatalistic and abandoning of any responsibility for their own welfare. There are several arguments against this view.

- Acknowledging the will of God or Allah does not mean an abandonment of personal responsibility, and indeed those who profess faith may have a moral duty under their faith to do their utmost to take responsibility for their own health.
- The realms of medical science and religious faith are arguably not the same. Medical science can tell us that in terms of Mendelian genetics, the off-spring of two parents who each carry an autosomal recessive gene have a one-in-four chance in each pregnancy of inheriting the major condition. But medical science cannot tell us why, in one family, three children in a row have the condition, whereas in another family no children have the condition. In such instances religion and science are addressing very different questions.
- There is increasing interest in the positive benefits of religion for health, although these may be through different mechanisms in different instances and indeed the benefits may be reversed in some circumstances. For example, Gabe and Thorogood (1986), in a small-scale study of minor tranquillizer use of White and African-Caribbean working class women in Hackney, found lower use of minor tranquillizers by the African-Caribbean women, who reported higher levels of social support associated with membership of their Christian churches. On the other hand, Hill (1994) found that while the Christian faith was found supportive by mothers of

disabled children on low incomes, exhortations based on scriptures were found to drain their coping resources. In still other instances reference to religious texts has been found to be beneficial.

Health beliefs

Health beliefs deriving from ethnic, cultural or religious world views might superficially be regarded as in opposition to rational scientific medicine. However, healthcare providers may well be familiar with the type of issue raised in consultations which may be characterised by the phrase 'How should I live my life?' While such a question may have elements of seeking technical medical information, it also clearly has social and moral dimensions. In thinking about such a fundamental question themselves, many patients may draw upon a complex mix of family example, economic necessity, and world view. However, those with a strong religious conviction may additionally have their faith as a central guiding force. Consider, for instance the place of a fatwa in Islam. In the UK media the term fatwa is most closely associated with the Salman Rushdie affair, and has acquired connotations of being a negative phenomenon. However, a fatwa, or a legal opinion expressed by an Islamic scholar, is more commonly a form of positive guidance to deal with complexities of how one should live one's life. The following is one example of a Muslim fatwa on a health issue.

Blood donation

It is permissible to donate and transfuse blood if:

- There is a desperate need to donate blood;
- There is no other alternative; and
- This has been prescribed by an expert medical practitioner.

This permissibility is based on the principal of 'necessity relaxes prohibition' (Al-Ashbaah). However, the permissibility of blood donation and blood transfusion is determined by the following conditions:

- The donor willingly donates his blood. If he is compelled to do so, it will not be permissible;
- There is no danger to his (the donor's) life or health;
- If the doctor feels that the patient will lose his life and there is no other alternative but recourse of blood transfusion; and
- There is no fear of death but the recovery is not possible without blood transfusion.

It is not permissible to sell one's blood or to pay the blood donor. However, if one is in need of blood desperately and the only means to obtain the blood is to purchase it, then it will be permissible to pay for the blood. Blood donation and blood transfusion is not permissible for the sake of beautification or for any other reason other than genuine necessity. (Desai, 2005).

Other health issues

By examining the types of issues about which one religious group asks life questions, we may be able to identify materials/substances that may cause problems (medicines containing gelatine, medicines with alcohol bases, medicines with animal sources, etc). Other issues pertinent to Muslims might include:

- Questions about contact with the opposite sex in various health settings (male doctors, male gynaecologists, female physiotherapists, female receptionists, male gynaecologists).
- Questions about ritual purity in preparation for prayers (unspecified discharge from private areas; fitting a stoma bag; slight stress incontinence leaking few drops of urine; problems with menstruation; passing of wind; being HIV positive or having AIDS).
- Questions about the acceptability of drugs within the religious faith (are tobacco, cannabis, mushrooms, creatine supplements, steroids, permitted)?
- Questions about the border lines between medical treatment and beauty enhancement (ie electrolysis to remove hair to help control eczema, an operation to improve the gums, medication to reduce male hormones and thereby reduce male hair loss, dyeing of hair, breast implants, liposuction, teeth braces, contact lenses).
- Questions about traditional treatments mentioned in scriptures (black seed oil; wearing of charms of written verses of the Qur'an or drinking water in which such verses have been submerged; vinegar, honey, olive oil and oiling the hair).
- Questions about what, in the professional division of labour in Western medicine, we might call mental health (advice on self-harm, on seeing an evil spirit, increased fear of and thoughts of death following a difficult childbirth).
- Questions about sexual relations (effects of masturbation, what methods of birth control are permissible, intercourse with husband when pregnant, acceptability of sterilisation where a woman fears pregnancy may trigger AIDS from her current HIV status).

- Questions about the acceptability of alternative or new practices such as reiki, yoga, or aerobics to music.
- Questions about approaching death (appropriateness of life support machines, of euthanasia, of living wills, of definitions of brain death, of 'do not resuscitate' instructions, of 'comfort care only' and of how to live with someone suffering with cancer or terminal illness).

The point about these is not to provide the health professional with a list of answers, because, in the case of Islam, it may be that different muftis (a person responsible for interpreting Muslim law, held in high esteem by the population) may provide different answers, that the answers themselves may leave some, or even considerable room for discretion based on the illness experience itself, and that in any case the answer taken up by the individual asking the question may not be in the manner in which other Muslims live their lives. However, the variety of questions cited can serve as an initial guide to the types of domains that patients from many backgrounds, and not just Islam, may find troubling.

Improving services for all patients

It will be clear by now that the approach we are suggesting to working with diversity does not consist of a list of easy answers, but depends largely on continuing negotiations with patients and their families. Indeed, we think that attending to the needs of minority ethnic clients may result in an improved service to all clients. This is because in reframing our service to attend to particular domains of interest, perhaps initially prompted by a growing awareness of diversity, we are then better placed to ask all patients about their preferences with regard to that domain. Below are just some areas where services for all patients might be improved.

Medication

A number of religions have particular proscriptions against consumption of certain products, particularly products derived from animal sources and products with an alcohol base. The importance of this is in inculcating an awareness that this is a domain of potential concern to all patients, rather than prompting rote learning of specific issues, ie pork products are forbidden to Jews and Muslims and beef products to Hindus. Patients concerned with animal welfare or who are vegetarians may also object to animal products, and such objections can only be ascertained by asking all patients. With respect to porcine products, the National Prescribing Centre publishes a book that lists porcine-derived drugs and their alternatives, and offers advice on involving patients with decisions on porcine-derived medicines (see: http://www.npc.co.uk/).

Clothing/jewellery

For some faiths or cultures, particular items of clothing, jewellery or body markings may carry a deep symbolic significance. For example, the multi-layered religious, historical and symbolic meanings of the steel bangle (kara) worn by Sikhs may mean that a patient would not wish to take off this item for medical treatment. The current trend for body-piercings and markings means that other patients should be consulted about their needs with respect to clothing and body ornaments. Consideration of these issues would improve the respect and care shown to all patients.

Washing

A number of cultures value free-flowing water for washing and regard baths as tantamount to sitting in dirty stagnant water, and, as such, are unsuitable for cleanliness. For example, some may require free-flowing water in the form of a bidet or a jug of water to wash themselves after toileting. Other issues include:

- notions that parts of the body require special cleanliness (the head, the hair);
- ideas that certain parts of the body are prone to dirtiness (the feet);
- notions that upper and lower parts of the body must not be cross-contaminated;
- notions that pets or contamination with animal hairs from pets is associated with uncleanliness;
- recognition that some bodily secretions are regarded as pure and others as polluted; and
- recognition of the relationship of bathing to prayer and to taking of meals.

Patients should therefore be asked their preferences about washing.

A model for thinking about culture

When faced with increasing ethnic diversity within society, the understandable reaction of many health professionals is to want to learn about pre-existing cultural beliefs. However well-intentioned this view may be, it has several important problems. These problems include ignoring diversities within cultures; underplaying the similarities between people of different cultures; ignoring the changing nature of cultures over time; not taking account of other relations of power such as gender relations and economic power; not conceiving of culture as nurturing or enabling as well as restricting; and not taking note of how material circumstances such as relative poverty or affluence both affect and are affected by culture. If culture is so complex and multi-factorial, how can community health professionals be expected to grasp all the details and nuances? It seems an impossible task, and hence we suggest an alternative for understanding culture. This understanding is based on a model of communicative relationships that uses the metaphor of masks to understand how people present themselves in social encounters.

This model derives from the work of Erving Goffman who uses the analogy of drama to bring understanding to human interactions, including interactions between health professionals and patients. In the medical literature, the model of interaction as a form of drama has been used to analyse encounters between GPs and drug company representatives (see Somerset et al, 2001). Goffman (1959) draws a distinction between what he calls our 'selves-in-the-world' (represented in *Figure 2.1* by the masks) and our true inner selves (represented in *Figure 2.1* by the shape lying behind the mask). What we present to others is the view of ourselves that we would like others to have of us. In presenting ourselves to the outside world, we draw upon our self 'behind the mask', but both the extent to which we do so, and the way in which we do so, depends upon the particular circumstances we find ourselves in. That is to say, we are creative in the manner in which we interact with others. We choose to display parts of who we are but to keep other aspects of our inner selves from view.

At the very least, we are capable of presenting a number of possible versions of our selves by choosing what to bring to the fore for the purposes of engaging with our doctor. Stimson and Webb (1975) apply this idea to the doctor–patient consultation. They point out that patients, despite the gap in power between themselves and the doctor, still have the capacity to withhold information from the doctor that is within their power to divulge should they wish. Patients could reveal to the doctor that they never took the prescription that was written for them to the pharmacist at all. They

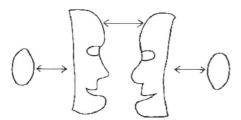

Figure 2.1:The interaction between health professional and patient conceived of as a drama-like encounter. From: Dyson and Brown (2006: 20). Material is reproduced with the kind permission of the Open University Press.

could say they frequently forgot to take their tablets, or that they made up for these lapses by taking double or triple doses at other times. They could say that they shared their drugs with a friend who had the same symptoms, or even that they used their drugs in ways never medically intended, such as to cheer themselves up. But they choose not to. Goffman (1959) no doubt had similar instances in mind when he wrote about the presentation of self in everyday life. The self-in-the-world is what patients put forward of themselves in any encounter, which may be a version of their inner self, their sense of themselves. The (inner) self is best thought of as a resource that can be drawn upon to construct the series of different versions of our selves; the suite of different presentations people give of themselves in everyday life.

However, this is not merely a question of a false public face and a true private one. When an actor puts on a mask, the purpose is not to conceal him or herself, but to transform him or herself. The self is not an inner essence, static and unchanging. It is itself continually under construction, modified sometimes dramatically in the process of encountering other selves-in-the-world. Our sense of ourselves changes in the process of interaction, and thus the resources out of which to construct our self-in-the-world are also constantly in flux.

Thus we might re-draw the encounter between the healthcare provider and the patient as shown in *Figure 2.2*.

Where does culture fit into all this? We might conceive of culture as the stock of resources that patients use to construct their sense of themselves and the self-in-the-world they put forward to their healthcare provider. In order to present their symptoms, to explain their health behaviours, to account for the other people such as family, friends and work colleagues, with all of whom they may or may not have checked out their ideas before coming to see the doctor, patients draw upon their culture. It is as if they are going to a library shelf or store cupboard to draw on the items they feel they need. However,

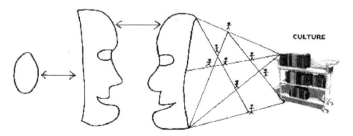

Figure 2.2:The interaction between healthcare provider and patient, with the patient drawing selectively on culture and taking up different identities in different contexts.

what is in the library or store cupboard is not fixed and unchanging. What is there partly depends upon material factors such as what can be afforded, and on availability. Other items become out of date and cease to be an active ingredient in that culture. Other new items come into stock as cultures change over time.

One final layer can be added to our understanding of culture. So far we have represented the inner self as if it were fixed. But just as culture is not fixed, nor is the self a single, unitary, rational, unchanging whole. In *Chapter 7* on mental health, we look at an example of how a particular group of patients think of the world in a way that is quite literally not self-centred in both the common form of that phrase (not selfish), and the sense that their thinking is grounded neither in a self-in the-world nor an inner self.

Key points

- There is diversity in the UK population in terms of country of birth, ethnicity and religion.
- The largest ethnic-religious grouping remains White Christians who comprised 36 million people or nearly 70% of the adult population of the UK in 2001.
- Some religious groups are relatively homogenous in terms of ethnicity (97% of British Jews are White)
- Some ethnic groups are relatively homogenous in terms of stated religion; 92% of British Pakistani people are Muslims.
- Other sources of diversity within ethno-religious groupings include gender, migrant status, reason for migration, generation, housing, language, socio-economic status, experience of racism, experience of health services and experience of other public services (education, social security, or housing).
- We cannot 'learn' cultures because they are numerous, diverse and change over time and according to different contexts.
- We can, however, identify 'domains of interest'; the domains around which patients may vary in their preferences and needs.
- Attending to variation around domains of interest, (including diet, medication, washing, personal ornaments) carries the possibility of improving health services to all patients, and not just those from minority ethnic groups.

References

Desai E (2005) Available from http://islam.tc/ask-imam/view.php?q=2440 [Accessed 26/10/2005]

Dyson SM, Brown B (2006) *Social Theory and Applied Health Research*. Milton Keynes: Open University Press,

Gabe J, Thorogood N (1986) Prescribed drug use and the management of everyday life. *Sociological Review* **34**(4): 737–72

Goffman E (1959) *The Presentation of Self in Everyday Life*. Harmondsworth: Penguin

Greenslade L, Madden M, Pearson M (1997) From visible to invisible: The 'problem' of the health of Irish people in Britain. In Marks L, Worboys M (eds) *Migrants, Minorities and Health*. pp. 147–78. London: Routledge

Gunaratnam Y (2001) Ethnicity and palliative care, In Culley L, Dyson SM (eds) *Ethnicity and Nursing Practice*. pp 169-185. Basingstoke: Palgrave

Healthcare Commission (2009) *Tackling the Challenge. Promoting Race Equality in the NHS in England*. Commission for Healthcare Audit and Inspection, London

Hill S (1994) *Managing Sickle Cell Disease in Low Income Families*. Philadelphia, PA: Temple University Press

Rendall MS, Ball DJ (2004) Immigration, em–igration and the ageing of the overseas-born population in the United Kingdom. *Population Trends* **116**: 18–27

Somerset M, Weiss M, Fahey T (2001) Dramaturgical study of meetings between general practitioners and representatives of pharmaceutical companies. *British Medical Journal* **323**:1481–4

Stimson G, Webb B (1975) *Going to See the Doctor*. London: Routledge and Kegan Paul

Further reading

Culley L (2000) Working with Diversity: Beyond the factfile. In: Davies C, Finlay L, Bullam A eds. *Changing Practice in Health and Social Care*. Sage, London: 131–42

Kelleher D, Hillier S (eds) (1996) *Researching Cultural Differences in Health*. Routledge, London

Office for National Statistics (2005). *Focus on Ethnicity and Identity*. Available from: www.statistics.gov.uk

CHAPTER 3

Managing diversity in healthcare practice

In this chapter, we examine some practical issues in responding to the challenges of providing healthcare in a multi-ethnic society. We start with outlining the legal context for equality work in the NHS and follow this with a discussion of issues relating to the organisational structures within which clinical practice is situated, including the issue of ethnic data collection and ethnic monitoring, and the policies necessary to challenge racism. We consider some practical suggestions for taking a medical history with patients whose first language is not English, and explore the increasing use of chaperones, especially for intimate examinations.

A legal framework for health services

The main legislative framework for current race equality measures in the UK is the Race Relations (Amendment) Act 2000 (Appendix 3.1). The crux of this legislation is that it places the onus on the service provider to take proactive steps in support of working with diverse communities. In a sense, the previous 1976 Race Relations Act was about avoiding negatives: avoiding direct racist discrimination and avoiding indirect (what we might now call unintentional) racist discrimination. Direct discrimination might include name-calling, or deliberately mistreating people because of the colour of their skin or their culture. Indirect discrimination is where a policy or practice is ostensibly applied universally, but where it has the effect of indirectly limiting the choices or possibilities of a particular ethnic group. For example, stating that employees can only take two weeks of annual leave consecutively discriminates against those who may have kinship obligations that require them to travel abroad to maintain family ties. The Race Relations (Amendment) Act 2000 breaks new ground in that it not only requires service providers actively to anticipate and avoid negative issues, but also requires them to actively engage in positive processes.

Single equality schemes

In addition to complying with the Race Relations (Amendment) Act 2000, public bodies are subject to the provisions of the Disability Discrimination Act 2005 and the Equality Act 2006. In recognition of this set of statutory duties, and anticipating further developments in relation to age, religion and sexual orientation, the Department of Health has pioneered a broad approach to health inequalities. Following the establishment of the Commission for Equality and Human Rights in October 2007 (replacing the Commission for Racial Equality, Equal Opportunities Commission and Disability Rights Commission), the Department of Health has championed the development of Single Equality Schemes (SES) which are based around six equality strands – race, gender, disability, age, sexual orientation, and religion and belief. The Department of Health (2007) has published its own SES for the period 2007–2010, and Primary CareTrusts (PCTs) are expected to develop a similar approach.

PCTs are expected to undertake an Equality Impact Assessment (EqIA) of all policies and functions and devise appropriate action plans. EqIAs are a way of examining the main policies and processes of an organisation to see whether they have the potential to affect people differently. Their purpose is to identify and address real or potential inequalities resulting from policy and practice development. An EqIA should cover all of the six strands of diversity. A step-by step guide to carrying out an EqIA is provided on the National Health Service (NHS) Employers' website (www.nhsemployers.org).

The NHS is the largest employer of minority ethnic people in the UK and workforce equality issues are also a key feature of the Department of Health Equality and Human Rights policy. Information and guidance on workforce issues is also provided by NHS Employers.

A web audit of NHS Trusts carried out by the Healthcare Commission in Spring 2007 (Healthcare Commission, 2009), found that only 9% (35 out of 394) of NHS trusts are publishing everything they are required to under the Race Relations Act 1976. From the 2007/2008 assessment year, Trusts failing to comply with the statutory publication requirements in respect of race and disability could face not meeting one of the Government's core standards for healthcare (Standard C7e). This could affect ratings in the annual health check.

Ethnic monitoring

To operate an effective equality scheme, it is vital to have robust ethnicity data. However, ethnic monitoring in primary care in particular is very patchy. Ethnic recording is the actual task of asking clients to complete a form to indicate their ethnic origin. However, ethnic monitoring is more than just collecting ethnic data, and to achieve quality ethnic monitoring, we need to:

- Collect data in appropriate categories (not categories based on nationality; country of birth or concepts based on inappropriate notions of 'race')
- Explain to the client the reason behind the collection of data in ethnic categories.
- Maintain these records over time and not just as a one-off initiative.
- Analyse patterns in the data to see if they reveal any possible inequities or unintended discrimination.
- Ensure that any discrimination revealed by monitoring such patterns is addressed promptly.
- Utilise the ethnic data collected in order to help plan appropriate services in the future.

The Department of Health requires use of the UK 2001 Census categories (see *Chapter 2*) for collecting in-patient data, and the use of such official categories has the advantage of permitting comparisons with the wide range of data derived from the 2001 Census. However, it is possible that the judicious use of extra categories to reflect particular local circumstances (for instance if the practice serves a number of families of Somali descent) may help in local ethnic monitoring. One development of the 2001 Census categories that we have found useful in our research is to recognise the increasing numbers of people of so-called 'mixed-race' or dual heritage by permitting people to self-allocate to the two (or more) categories with which they identify, and in any combination, not just those restricted few offered by the 2001 Census categories (see Dyson et al, 2006). Practices wishing to capture data on new migrant communities, such as those from the EU, will need to extend the Census categories.

The primary purpose of ethnic monitoring must be to identify and address any discriminatory patterns. Sometimes this may reveal direct or indirect discrimination per se, but sometimes the pattern will consist of the identification of a puzzle in need of explanation. The relative lack of use of palliative care services in a particular group might be because of the younger age structure of the minority ethnic populations the practice serves. However, it might equally be because the practice has not developed culturally competent services and/or has not consulted community members about their preferences for addressing care of the dying. It is therefore important to recognise that identifying an association between an ethnic group and a service is the beginning of the process (recognising there is an issue that requires addressing) and that ethnicity in and of itself does not constitute an explanation.

Indeed, in terms of service development, it is important not to reduce everything to ethnicity, since what is more important in overall community health needs assessment is to have information that is fit for purpose. In terms of preparing information leaflets, for example, it is the language read (if any) that is required. In relation to providing interpretation services, or developing bilingual reception and nursing staff, we need to collect information on the language spoken, not ethnicity.

> **GOOD PRACTICE: Ethnic monitoring**
>
> Ethnicity data has been included in the Patient Profiling Project initiated at Central Liverpool PCT. A questionnaire collects data including ethnic classification, language use, literacy and socio-economic status, as well as lifestyle choices, health and ill health experience and patient satisfaction. This has been commended by the Commission for Race Equality as the Gold Standard for ethnic monitoring in Primary Care. Ninety eight practices are now collecting this information, many from newly registered patients.
>
> See: http://www.nwpho.org.uk/reports/ethnic%20health%20RE-lay.pdf

Working with a diverse patient population

A health professional may clearly come across many different cultures and sub-cultures in clinical practice, and what is therefore needed is not a list of cultural 'traits' of different groups, but a structure that can help increase cultural competencies across a wide range of possible circumstances, without falling into the opposite trap of 'treating everyone equally'. The following is a series of suggestions for working with diversity in healthcare,

The ethos of the practice

Start and maintain, by regular updating, a list of local community contacts. These could include self-help groups, voluntary organisations based in the area, faith-based groups, alternative practitioners (for example, ayurvedic healers and hakims, as well as acupuncturists and chiropractors), community centres, or a major local business employer. Visit the organisations or the people to find out more about them. It may be that in some cases you want to be able to refer clients to them, or encourage the organisations to refer clients to you. It may be that you have some concerns about what you find. In any event, you will develop a fuller understanding of the wider network of local influences within which your clients make sense of their health and illness.

Try to make the wider ethos of the practice reflect the diversity of communities you serve. Signs and information leaflets available in numerous languages, and more informal reading material in the waiting room could also be linguistically appropriate. Where there is a television monitor in the waiting room, this could be used to play tapes explaining the practice services available and how to access them, or health education messages in relevant community languages.

You will need to anticipate the possibility that a client may be accompanied by a group of family members or friends. Rather than saying this is unacceptable because the patient is an individual and the provider–patient relationship is sacrosanct, this 'group' orientation to health, which is a characteristic of some cultures, must be respected at all times. However, this requires you to undertake the difficult task of determining with the client the appropriateness of context. Determining whether or not the client is content with a group presence, especially as this requires the client to answer in confidence, is a challenge, especially if the client does not understand much English. The group presence is appropriate for some consultations and not others, or may be appropriate for part of the consultation, or for some members of the group but not for other group members. 'Best practice' then becomes the outcome of difficult negotiations with clients rather than the application of specific pre-determined protocols.

Taking a medical history

The following factors should be considered when helping the client communicate their medical history.

- Learn a specific phrase to greet the patient in their first language.
- Learn the way in which the patient prefers to be addressed.
- Learn the correct pronunciation of their name.
- Identify a date of birth, but also whether the calendar year and/or the day and month are estimates.
- Use the six 'W's in formulating questions: who, why, where, when, what and which. Questions formed using these terms need a basic understanding of the question in order to be able to provide an answer. If the patient cannot answer questions framed in this way, there is a good chance they may not have understood the question.
- Avoid asking compound questions (two questions in one).
- Avoid asking questions framed in the negative (because it is then unclear whether the answer yes refers to 'yes it is' or 'yes it is not').
- Avoid leading questions (questions that contain within them a hint as to the expected or desired answer).
- Avoid 'small talk'. If the person is having difficulty understanding,

they may not appreciate using scarce emotional energy in translating phrases of little help in getting better.

- If the patient does not understand, re-phrase the question using different words rather than repeat the question.
- If the consultation requires an interpreter, but none is available, note the lack of interpreter and the uncertainty of information as part of record-keeping. Try to repeat the consultation at a time when an interpreter is available.

Countering racist harassment in primary care

One key feature establishing the ethos of an organisation such as a healthcare practice is the public demonstration of the willingness to challenge racism, and the organisational structures to ensure that this is carried out. The former Commission for Racial Equality made the following recommendations for addressing racism in primary care settings.

- It is important to identify the perpetrators, both because of the seriousness of the offence, and because it shows that racial harassment will not be tolerated.
- Cases should be monitored carefully, and appropriate case notes and witness statements prepared on individual incidents.
- In certain circumstances, the police should be contacted.
- Disciplinary action should be taken if the perpetrator is a member of staff. Where he or she is a patient, the sanctions might include restrictions on attendance at a particular health clinic, or removing the patient altogether from the practitioner's list.
- A proper complaints procedure should be drawn up, incorporating an anti-racial harassment strategy. The basic elements of the strategy should include:
  - Providing advice and information.
  - Making arrangements to liaise with the relevant agencies, such as: the Department of Health, police, law centres, and voluntary agencies.
  - Producing information and publicity material, in all the relevant languages, on the help available to patients and the local community.

Patient records

One issue that a culturally competent service will need to develop is a naming system within patient records that can adequately reflect the full range of naming systems used by the populations served. This also has implications for ongoing education of all who may need to access and update the same records. The following fields need to be incorporated in the patient records.

- An appropriate number of fields for family names, given names, personal names, and auspicious names (such as Singh [lion] or Kaur [princess] in Sikh naming systems).
- A field for a phonetic description of how to pronounce the names accurately.
- A field for how the patient would like to be addressed by practice staff.
- A field for linking the patient to other blood family members.
- A field for which letter of the alphabet should determine filing order.
- An accurate date of birth and a rider if this date of birth is an estimate.

One way we may try to give people a unique identification is by their date of birth. However, a diminishing number of older generations may not have a fixed birth date, perhaps because they migrated from a rural area of their country where paper records were not the norm. They may therefore be offering merely an estimate of their birth date when asked (for example, January 1st). If this estimate changes on different occasions unwary health workers may be mistaken in thinking they have seen several different people rather than one person, or if people share the same name and give the same arbitrary birth date, that they have seen the same person. This is one of a number of cautionary principles that should be borne in mind when taking of a medical history from the patient.

Chaperones

The use of chaperones for patients undergoing intimate examinations by their family doctor illustrates a number of issues in the social practice of healthcare. First, the precipitating reason for the use of chaparones may not be the reason for its continuance or growth. For instance it might plausibly be argued that a fear of misunderstanding, or litigation, may have been a substantial initial impetus to the use of chaperones. Second, the development of chaperones may have been initially prompted by a desire to address perceived 'cultural differences' between the expectations of different ethnic groups in their relations with professionals. However, the ultimate consequence of developing chaperone services may be to question traditional medical practice and indeed to improve such practice for all patients. The experiences of two Irish women certainly suggest this is the case:

> *I think this is not only a very necessary move for the protection of both patient and doctor, but it is also recognising that such examinations are*

extremely personal and a woman might feel more comfortable having another female present. Male doctors, for far too long, have expected women to submit to such invasive procedures without a second thought. You might be doing it every day lads, but for every woman lying on that couch, it's HER personal parts, she's probably dying of embarrassment and don't forget – it just might be her first time!

It is mandatory for male doctors to have a female nurse present when they perform any intra-vaginal procedure. The patient must also have the right to have a companion of her choice present. Chaperones apart, patients should be draped and gowned. They should have private space to change in and out of their clothes. The doctor should also explain the procedure beforehand. Regular visits and familiarity are not reasons to overlook these courtesies.

From: http://www.irishhealth.com/?level=4andid=6915
[Accessed 6 December 2005]

The medical Royal Colleges, the General Medical Council, and the medical defence organisations now recommend that intimate examinations are not carried out by unaccompanied doctors.

Rosenthal et al (2005) surveyed over 1200 general practitioners in England about the use of chaperones during intimate examinations. A total of 517 (68%) male GPs and 24 (5%) female GPs usually or always offered a chaperone, while 410 (54%) males and 9 (2%) females usually or always used a chaperone. Only 60 males (8%) never used one compared to 344 (70%) females. The use of chaperones was associated with increasing age, belonging to a non-White ethnic group, and working in a smaller practice.

Practice nurses were the most common chaperones, but a non-clinical member of the practice staff, a student or GP registrar, or another doctor, were alternatives.

Use of chaperones by male doctors has substantially increased since the 1980s and 1990s, but use by female doctors remains low, despite one third of practices having a policy. Record keeping about offering and using chaperones is poor, and significant barriers, such as confidentiality and time constraints, still exist. More flexible guidance is needed for general practice as well as further research into patients' views and wishes on the use of chaperones.

As this research suggests, the use of chaperones seems to be increasing within medical practice, although their use also raises questions, such as does the chaperone sit within or remain outside of any screens drawn around the examining table. The answer to such questions remains with the process of negotiating care with the individual patient.

> **Key points**
>
> - The Race Relations (Amendment) Act 2000 and the development of Single Equality Schemes provide many opportunities for improving service delivery for minority ethnic users.
> - Ethnic monitoring is more than just collecting ethnic data. It involves a commitment to use the data to combat discrimination and inequities.
> - Establishing an ethos that the practice is attuned to the diversity of the population it serves can help in underpinning good patient care.
> - Practices need to have robust policies on countering racism and to make those policies transparent and public.
> - Patient records need to be based on sufficient fields to accommodate the full range of naming systems of different ethnic groups.
> - There are a number of cautionary principles to guide the taking of a medical history from the patient.
> - Chaperones may improve care for all patients, not just those from a minority ethnic group. Use of chaperones represents the beginning of negotiating issues of modesty in care with the patient and not the final resolution of the issue.

References

Commission for Racial Equality (2006) http://www.cre.gov.uk/gdpract/health_care_cop_ harass.html [accessed 15 June 2006]

Department of Health (2005) Practical Guide to Ethnic Monitoring in the NHS and Social Care. London: Department of Health

Department of Health (2007) Single Equality Scheme 2007–2010. London: Department of Health

Dyson SM, Culley LA, Gill C, Hubbard S, Kennefick A, Morris P, Rees D, Sutton F, Squire P (2006) Ethnicity Questions and Antenatal Screening for Sickle Cell/Thalassaemia [EQUANS] in England: A randomized controlled trial of two questionnaires. Ethnicity and Health 11(2): 169–89

Healthcare Commission (2009) Tackling the Challenge. Promoting Race Equality in the NHS in England. Commission for Healthcare Audit and Inspection, London

Further reading

Ali S, Atkin K (eds) (2004) *Primary Healthcare and South Asian Populations. Meeting the Challenges.* Radcliffe Medical Press, Abingdon

Thompson N (2003) *Promoting Equality. Challenging Discrimination and Oppression.* Palgrave Macmillan, Basingstoke

Equality and Human Rights Commission. The duty to promote race equality. Performance guidelines for health organisations. www.equalityhumanrights.com

Appendix 3.1

Race Relations (Amendment) Act 2000

The 2000 Race Relations (Amendment) Act places an onus on public bodies in the UK, to develop 'race equality schemes'. This should provide primary care services in the UK with the impetus to overcome institutional racism by developing robust equal opportunities policies on ethnicity. Under such Race Equality Schemes, public authorities will have to:

(1) Assess whether their functions and policies are relevant to race equality. There are clearly a number of ways in which health services are related to 'race' equality. The main ways include: (i) How does the NHS respond to the material deprivations underpinning the unequal health statuses of many from minority ethnic groups in the UK? And (ii) How do healthcare providers ensure that care is based on equitable treatment, that is on treatment that results in all groups benefiting from services in a way that is commensurate with their needs, and not merely on equal treatment, that is treatment in which everyone receives the same service, irrespective of their different levels of need?

(2) Monitor their policies to see how they affect race equality. This suggests that an assessment of healthcare provision will require assessment for their respective impacts on different ethnic groups. Such assessments might reasonably be expected to include, for example, (i) collecting data on ethnicity, religion and language needs of the population served, (ii) monitoring consultation levels, referral rates to secondary and tertiary care, referral rates to specialist services, rates of usage of community health services such as health visiting, district nursing services, well person clinics, (iii) monitoring levels and types of drugs prescribed, (iv) an evaluation of the provision of bilingual nurses or professional interpreters to ensure equal opportunity of informed consent for tests and (v) an evaluation of any differences in choices provided to clients of different ethnic groups.

(3) Assess and consult on policies they are proposing to introduce. The act of researching need and consulting about policies can itself help in the delivery of services. This is because the channels of communication that have to be established in order to make consultation anything more than tokenism are themselves the channels that need to be established to deliver culturally relevant services. Let us take a simple example. To consult effectively and equitably, the consultation must be in the preferred language of the client. In solving the challenge of consultation a number of aspects need to be addressed:

- How many people prefer to be consulted in which written/spoken languages, bearing in mind that not all will be able to read and write their first language;
- Which clients are integrated by virtue of participation in community groups (membership of faith-based groups; ethnic-specific community centres; schools-based groups; business-based groups; sports-based groups; parents groups, groups of elders, groups for specific medical conditions, philanthropic charity groups) and which clients are outside of such formally identifiable community groupings?
- Do people understand the notion of a community consultation, do they have the skills to engage in it, and do they have the confidence to assert their needs?

(4) Publish the results of their consultations, monitoring and assessments. In attending to this provision, healthcare providers would need to know the media most relevant to local clients, and anticipating the ongoing requirement of provision (5), below, to continue to communicate effectively with the public.

(5) Ensure the public have access to the information and services they provide. These three latter requirements of the Act (3)–(5) provide local health services with the impetus to develop appropriate pathways for consulting, publishing for, and communicating with their local communities. The challenge here is to move beyond the traditional and tokenistic consultation of the 'organised', that is those using a key service such as a place of worship or a community centre. Nor are 'community elders' necessarily any more representative of their communities than 'community youngsters', whom consultation traditionally leaves out of account.

(6) Train their staff on the new duties. This requirement implies not only a familiarisation with the key components of the Act itself, but a range of skills that different personnel within primary care may need to develop. These might include skills of research methods, service evaluation and service audit in order to successfully carry out ethnic monitoring. These might involve skills in community health needs assessment in order to consult effectively with communities served. It might entail recognising and valuing skills: for example, paying extra grades and increments for staff who can effectively communicate in relevant community languages.

CHAPTER 4

Language and communication support

The failure to provide adequate support for those whose first language is not English is one of the most common problems identified in research studies on ethnic inequalities in accessing healthcare. In this chapter, we look more closely at some of the issues involved in communication support.

There are no official sources of comprehensive information for the UK population on main spoken languages and competency in English (Apsinall, 2007) and so there is little reliable information on numbers of people who need language support in the NHS. Most European countries, the USA, Canada, Australia, New Zealand and South Africa include questions on language in their national censuses. This is not the case in the UK and many of the major Government health and social surveys, e.g. the General Household Survey, and most NHS user experience surveys do not ask about languages spoken or English language ability. Currently only two of the National Service Frameworks (diabetes and older people) incorporate language into their standards (Aspinall, 2007). The Office for National Statistics has recently announced that a question on main language spoken will be included in the next Census (2011). This will hopefully ease the process of incorporating language spoken into ethnic monitoring and routine data collection and provide comprehensive data on local population needs which is essential for world class commissioning.

Estimates of the numbers of people in England who have difficulties in English vary from around 400000 to 1.7 million. One study estimates that just 15% of Bengalis, 44% of Gujeratis and 29% of Punjabis would reach 'survival competence' (Carr-Hill et al, 1996). A recent report suggests that one in seven people from ethnic minorities faces language barriers in accessing public services. Language needs are identified as a key driver of social exclusion (Office of the Deputy Prime Minister, 2005) and this is increasingly recognised as a major obstacle in the effective delivery of health care. A study of the Vietnamese community in South London, for example, demonstrated the negative impact of communication difficulties (Free et al, 1999). Participants did not know about general practitioner out-of-hours arrangements, many were dependent on other people in gaining access to services and some had used 999 services inappropriately. Confusion regarding medicine and health advice were also experienced.

NHS Direct's interpreting facilities cover an extensive range of languages. However, these are considerably under-used and several surveys among minority ethnic respondents have shown that there is lower awareness of NHS Direct compared with the general population (Apsinall, 2007)

Language needs are often a priority for older populations of migrant origin. However, there is a constantly changing picture with the migration of new groups, including asylum seekers, refugees and new 'economic' migrants from Eastern Europe. Data collected in 1994 show the importance of age and gender in language fluency. Only about half of Pakistani and one quarter of Bangladeshi women aged between 25 and 44 years speak English well and only 4% of older Bangladeshi women are relatively fluent in English (see *Table 4.1*). Those who are aged over 25 when they come to Britain are the least likely to be able to speak or understand English.

London has become one of the most linguistically diverse cities in the world and it is thought that more than 300 languages are spoken by children in London schools (see *Table 4.2*). Although English remains overwhelmingly the most common first language, for more than one third of children it is not the language they will speak or hear spoken at home.

Ethnic monitoring and language needs

Primary care practices can gain estimates of languages spoken from a number of sources, but it is preferable for this information to be collected on registration and flagged on patient records.

It is important when considering language needs to remember that:

- Patients may understand English but find speaking it or reading it much more difficult.

Table 4.1. English spoken 'fluently' or 'fairly well'				
	Women age 25–44	**Women age 45–64**	**Men age 25–44**	**Men age 45–64**
Indian	73%	53%	88%	68%
African Asian	92%	71%	94%	87%
Pakistani	47%	28%	81%	56%
Bangladeshi	27%	4%	75%	54%
Chinese	82%	47%	82%	50%
Source: Adapted from Modood et al (1997)				

Table 4.2. The 40 most common first languages for children in London

Language	Approx total	Language	Approx total
English	608500	Igbo (Nigeria)	1900
Bengali and Sylheti	40400	French-based Creoles	1800
Punjabi	29800	Tagalog (Filipino)	1600
Gujarati	28600	Kurdish	1400
Hindi/Urdu	26000	Polish	1500
Turkish	15600	Swahili	1000
Arabic	11000	Lingala (Congo)	1000
English-based Creoles	10700	Albanian	900
Yorubu (Nigeria)	10400	Luganda (Uganda)	800
Somali	8300	Ga (Ghana)	800
Cantonese	6900	Tigrinya (Sudan)	800
Greek	6300	German	800
Akan (Ashanti)	6000	Japanese	800
Portuguese	6000	Serbian/Croatian	700
French	5600	Russian	700
Spanish	5500	Hebrew	650
Tamil (Sri Lanka)	3700	Korean	550
Farsi (Persian)	3300	Pashto (Afganistan)	450
Italian	2500	Amharic (Ethiopia)	450
Vietnamese	2400	Sinhala (Sri Lanka)	450

Numbers have been rounded up or down to the nearest 50

Source: http://www.nationalliteracytrust.org.uk/Research/lostop3.html#tongue [Accessed 13 June 2006]

- Patients may not be literate in their 'mother tongue'.
- Patients may be embarrassed to reveal their lack of understanding of English and so reject offers of interpretation or appear to indicate understanding even though this is in fact limited.
- Illness, stress, pain and anxiety can impinge upon a patient's ability to speak or understand English.
- Patients may have concerns about confidentiality and will need reassurance of the professional nature of any interpreting service.

- Patients may sometimes prefer to have a close family member to translate for them and this requires careful and sensitive consideration.

Effective communication is central to informed consent, service quality and patient safety. Despite substantial evidence in favour of providing proper language support there is a lack of consistent, universal provision or adequate resourcing of such services in the NHS. This is likely to come under increasing challenge following the implementation of the Race Relations (Amendment) Act 2000 and will be an issue which should be addressed in an Equality Impact Assessment. It is likely that communication support will be part of Care Quality Commission audits.

Many of the methods used to overcome communication problems in primary care involve a compromise in standards of privacy, confidentiality, accuracy and thoroughness. Clinical care can easily be compromised without adequate language support: a proper history cannot be taken; symptoms or problems can easily be missed or misinterpreted; expensive and unnecessary tests can be carried out; inappropriate treatments may be prescribed; and patient adherence may be reduced.

The use of 'informal interpreters' such as children and other family members can be very problematic.

Working with an interpreter

Using professional interpreters brings many benefits to the consultation/ treatment encounter (better accuracy, greater concordance, less stress for patient and provider) and may be a legal requirement under the Race Relations (Amendment) Act. Working with an interpreter, however, requires careful preparation and management, and it is advisable for healthcare teams to have some training in supporting interpreters. Good selection, training and management of interpreters is needed if the difficulties of handling sessions are to be minimised.

Policy

Try to arrange professional development time with the interpreter(s) so that you can all discuss the best ways to work together and, where possible plan the interview with the patient in advance. Allow about twice the length of time for a patient interview when using an interpreter, otherwise the communication advantages you gain through the interpretation may be lost through an over-rushed consultation. Involve the interpreting team in any continuing professional education or in any change of practice policy (e.g. on arrangements for home visits or making appointments).

Before the encounter

If possible, make time for the interpreter to discuss the aims of the encounter with the patient and prepare the interpreter for any technical information. Allow time for interpreters to introduce themselves and explain their role to the patients and to yourself. Check that interpreters actually speak the patient's language and dialect (e.g. people who speak one dialect do not necessarily speak another). Think about where interpreters can position themselves so as best to facilitate communication and to maintain the physical privacy of the patient.

Think about how the discussion should be arranged to ensure confidentiality of the encounter. You need to be aware that sometimes there are no equivalent words or expressions for health terms and indeed for body parts. In many languages, for example, there are no socially acceptable words for male or female genitalia or sexual activity and interpreters will have to find other ways of explaining what they mean. They will also have to deal with their own and the patient's embarrassment.

Think critically about the power relationship between you, the interpreters and the patients. In particular, be aware that an interpreter and a patient, although speaking the same language, may have been on opposing sides of a bitter ethnic/religious/political divide in a civil war from which they have both fled.

During the encounter

Encourage the interpreter to ask for clarification if he or she is unsure of your intended message and break up what you say into manageable chunks. Encourage interpreters to declare their personal views/beliefs so that all parties can be clear of the needs of the patient (as opposed to the healthcare provider or the interpreter). Encourage the interpreter to help you understand nuances of the patient's cultural context that may not be obvious to you and make sure that you avoid technical jargon or abbreviations. Avoid using colloquial or idiomatic expressions as the concepts may not transfer to other languages or cultures. Lastly, sit facing the patient and speak directly to him or her.

Afterwards

It is helpful after a consultation to discuss the session with the interpreter.

Using family members: What can go wrong?

A number of problems may arise in using a family member as an interpreter. These include:

- Mistranslations, misunderstandings and omissions: Several studies have shown an alarming level of such errors (Szczepura, 2005).
- Bias and distortion: Family members may have their own ideas about the situation and may not provide a translation of the health professional's views.
- Embarrassment: Family members and patients may be very embarrassed by some questions or procedures. This may inhibit reporting of problems (even between husband and wife in some cultures).
- Confidentiality: Many patients do not want family members to hear some information. Using non-family members is even more problematic, especially where there is a stigma attached to the condition (e.g. infertility, mental illness).
- Using children: Not only are the above problems likely to be more acute when using children as interpreters, there is the danger of long-term harm to the parent–child relationship. Children are given knowledge and responsibility that they should not have. In many cases children do not speak both languages equally well and using children as interpreters also often means keeping them from school.

Cultural sensitivity and empathy with those who need interpretation is very important, and this may be one advantage of using informal interpreters in some cases. It is important to offer professional interpretation. However, if the patient chooses to have an informal interpreter, it is very important to ensure that they are able to undertake this task effectively.

If you have to work with informal interpreters, there are a number of ways that problems can be minimised:

- Determine the interpreter's relationship to the patient: Patients may bring someone along simply because they are desperate, but their relationship with the interpreter may affect what you can ask to be translated.
- Determine the interpreter's command of English. It is often wise to communicate only essential/urgent information and wait until a trained interpreter is available.
- Try to determine if the interpreter fully understands or is able to translate your questions. Interpreters may themselves have limited English.

Health Scotland have produced an excellent guide for healthcare staff called *Now We're Talking. Interpreting Guidelines for Staff of NHS Scotland* (NHS Scotland 2008). The Chartered Institute of Linguists has published a checklist for selecting a translator. See www.iol.org.uk

Telephone interpretation

Telephone services such as Language Line can offer the advantage of 24-hour access to interpreting services and thus might be particularly useful for out-of-hours provision and where demand for interpreter services is generally low. For patients speaking rarely encountered languages this may be the only viable option. Use of video equipment can overcome some of the disadvantages of telephone interviewing but requires investment in equipment. Collaboration between practices can provide more comprehensive and cost-effective services.

> **GOOD PRACTICE: Interpretation**
>
> Cambridgeshire has developed CINTRA, a single service to cover all public service interpreting needs. This is a not-for-profit service set up by health and local authorities and is managed by community representatives and public service users.
>
> *http://www.colc.co.uk/cambridge/cintra/about.htm*

Translated information

Health information and health promotion materials need to be culturally as well as linguistically appropriate. This means that direct translations of existing material may not be suitable for all communities. Studies show that minority groups are eager for health promotion advice, but have poor uptake. People may not be literate in their 'mother tongue' and it may be necessary to move away from providing just printed materials and provide audiotape, CD, DVD and internet-based resources. Combinations of verbal, written and multi-media messages are likely to prove more effective than translated leaflets alone.

However, there is also some evidence that even such resources, without active outreach and support, show little advantage over written materials, although there is a serious lack of evaluative intervention studies. Information alone is rarely sufficient to guarantee effectiveness of health promotion activities in either minority or ethnic majority communities. Cultural beliefs and values play a considerable role in shaping health information-seeking behaviours. While some communities may prefer to rely on medical journals and the internet, others may prefer person-to-person communication with physicians and socially significant others.

A cultural competence model of health promotion involves a community-level focus, recognising the community and family context, informal health care support systems and the meaningful involvement of the community in developing and providing health promotion activities. It is also important in this model to determine community needs and tackle these first.

A wide range of translated material relevant to primary care is now available from a number of sources.

- Harpweb (www.harpweb.org.uk) is a good starting point.
- The NHS Evidence – ethnicity and health (www.library.nhs.uk/ ethnicity/) catalogues all the best currently available electronic evidence relating to healthcare for minority ethnic groups in Britain.
- Diversity Health Institute Clearing House (www.dhi.gov.au/ clearinghouse/Resources.htm). This Australian website lists an extensive range of resources on multicultural health, including fact sheets, reports, videos, CDs, journals, leaflets, posters and signs. Links are provided where possible so that resources can be accessed directly. A wide range of topics is covered including: ageing, child and youth health, cultural competence, disability, diseases and

GOOD PRACTICE: Translated information

Diabetes: Diabetes UK has produced a range of information and resources in Gujurati, Urdu, Hindi, Bengali, Punjabi, Chinese, Arabic and Somali which are also culturally appropriate, some of which are also available on tape. www.diabetes.org.uk. There is also helpful information for health professionals working with minority ethnic communities.

Hepatitis C: The Department of Health's *FaCe It Campaign* has produced a music CD for the South Asian community. The CD features advice from healthcare professionals and an interview conducted by TV health presenter Yasmin Qureshi with Shabana Begum, a Pakistani woman who recounts her experience of hepatitis C. The CD also features music from popular Asian artists. The CD has been distributed via Asian businesses, organisations and melas and is available in English and Urdu. The CD aims to improve understanding of how the virus is transmitted, diagnosed, treated and prevented.

conditions, drugs and alcohol, health promotion, men's health, mental health, new and emerging communities, refugee health and women's health.

- Multikulti (www.multikulti.org.uk) provides culturally appropriate and accurately translated information in welfare law, debt, employment, housing, immigration and welfare benefits as well as health. The health-related materials cover a wide range of topics, including caring for someone coming out of hospital; understanding depression; registering with a general practitioner; specialist NHS treatment and hospital services; postnatal depression; autism; post-traumatic stress; Asperger's syndrome; ectopic pregnancy; sexually transmitted diseases and many more.

- The New South Wales Multicultural Health Communication Service (http://www.mhcs.health.nsw.gov.au/index.html) provides a wide range of translated health materials. Although located in Australia this site has much of relevance to the UK and its minority ethnic groups.

Advocacy

Advocacy is intended to further the interests of the service user. Health advocates may or may not act as interpreters. If they perform this dual role, they should be sufficiently trained in interpretation. They may, however, be in a better position to address gaps in cultural understanding, and may be especially useful in areas with substantial refugee populations where they may be able to support individuals with a range of needs which are not just health related, but nevertheless impact on health.

Standards for cultural and linguistic competence

Services need to be both linguistically and culturally appropriate. Messages need to be tailored to the audience, with account taken of religious and cultural beliefs and practices as well as language needs (see *Chapters 1 and 2*). Standards for such provision have been developed in the US and include standards for culturally competent care and language access services, and organisational support for cultural competence (see www.omhrc.gov). Guidance on developing local communication support strategies has been published by the Department of Health: Equality and Human Rights Group (2004).

Key points

- Patients with limited proficiency in English are considerably disadvantaged in the British healthcare system.
- Providing language support is not time limited; the growth of globalised communities may mean increased need. Patient profile data must include language needs.
- Obtaining a professional interpreter is the beginning of the process, not the end. Training is needed for healthcare professionals in the use of language support.
- Not everyone who speaks a particular language will be literate in that language. Health promotion and information materials may need to be in spoken/visual form as well in written form.
- Translated information needs to be culturally as well as linguistically appropriate. Simply translating existing English language text may be inadequate.
- Evidence suggests that a community development model, with peer educators who have both linguistic competence and are culturally familiar with the target audience can be a successful approach to promoting health.

References

Aspinall P (2007) Language ability: A neglected dimension in the profiling of populations and health service users. *Health Education Journal* **66**(1): 90–106

Carr-Hill R, Passingham S, Wolf A, Kent N (1996) *Lost Opportunities: The Language Skills of Linguistic Minorities in England and Wales*. London: The Basic Skills Agency

Department of Health Equality and Human Rights Group (2004) Guidance on Developing Local Communication Support Services and Strategies. Download from www.dh.gov.uk

Office of the Deputy Prime Minister (2005) I*mproving Services, Improving Lives: Evidence and Key Themes. A Social Exclusion Unit Interim Report*. London: ODPM

Modood T, Berhoud R, Lakey J, Nazroo J, Smith P, Virdee S, Beishon S (1997) *Ethnic Minorities in Britain: Diversity and Disadvantage. The Fourth National Survey of Ethnic Minorities*. London: Policy Studies Institute

Free C, White P, Shipman C, Dale J (1999) Access to and use of out-of-hours services by members of Vietnamese community groups in South London: A focus group study. *Family Practice* **16**(4): 369–74

Szczepura A (2005) *An overview of the Research Evidence on Ethnicity and Communication in Health Care*. Centre for Evidence in Ethnicity, Health and Diversity, University of Warwick

Further reading

Centre for Evidence in Ethnicity, Health and Diversity (CEEHD) (2005) An Overview of the Research Evidence on Ethnicity, Communication and Healthcare. Available at: http://www2.warwick.ac.uk/fac/med/research/csri/ethnicityhealth/research

Henley A, Schott J (eds) (1999) *Culture, Religion and Patient Care in a Multi-Ethnic Society.* Age Concern. Part Three: Communication, London: 249–325

Mir G (2007) *Effective Communication with Service Users.* Race Equality Foundation, London

CHAPTER 5

Specific conditions

In this chapter, we take a number of key areas of disease and consider how ethnicity and culture play a part in helping us to understand the distinction between a disease state, such as heart disease, diabetes and hypertension, and an illness experience, in which patients may blend together in complex ways their own interpretation of technical knowledge, local folklore, advice of family and friends, and spiritual guidance.

Heart disease

Patterns of heart disease clearly differ among minority ethnic groups, as can be seen in *Figure 5.1*. Health professionals will wish to pay particular attention to their patients from groups with high relative risks of disease, and implement checks, monitoring and referrals as appropriate. However, this is not the same as saying that it is the patient's ethnicity that places them at greater risk of heart disease, and neither is it the same as saying that their ethnicity causes high rates of heart disease.

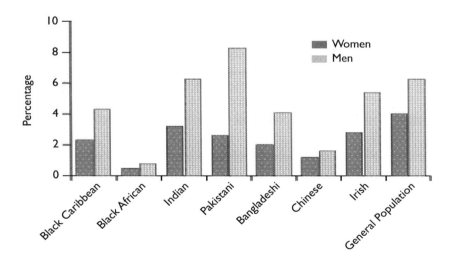

Figure 5.1. Prevalence of ischaemic heart disease within minority ethnic groups. From: Sprotson and Mindell (2006).

As *Figure 5.1* shows, there is considerable heterogeneity within the category 'minority ethnic' and within the groups which are commonly said to make up the 'South Asian' population. There are also important differences between rates for men and women both within and across ethnic groups.

It is perhaps not surprising that heart disease has been so problematic with respect to the care of some minority ethnic groups in the UK, since the analysis of heart disease in the broader population has long been fraught with controversy. For example, early health education campaigns have been criticised for placing too great an emphasis when explaining inequalities in heart disease on smoking, exercise and diets high in saturated fats. In fact these factors, taken together, explain less than 30% of observed differences between higher and lower income civil servants in the same work environment (Rodmell and Watt, 1986). This has led commentators to look at the roles of social support, social networks and place in social hierarchies as more plausible contributors to the majority of observed differences between groups in heart disease. Thus while advice on smoking, diet and exercise are of clear potential benefit, the public's notion that heart disease is related to social stress is actually more perceptive than the lifestyle issues that, historically, have been the focus of individual health education advice.

Wilkinson (1996) has shown that a major unexplored cause of conditions such as heart disease and diabetes is the release of substances such as adrenalin. People from minority ethnic groups may have little control over the flow and pace of their work, they may have to defer to those in authority or those who abuse them from whom they may be unable to seek redress, in other words be unable to fight or flee. In these circumstances adrenalin and similar substances are released for long rather than short periods, released without being dissipated, or released frequently rather than rarely, and the damaging effects of such substances in contributing to diabetes and heart disease, will be exacerbated.

The role of social and economic factors such as the experience of poverty and racism in heart disease has been underplayed in healthcare research. Rather such research has focused on issues such as a possible genetic basis to heart disease, and on the notion that having a family history of heart disease may be a risk factor in developing heart disease oneself. However, although both patients and health professionals may share in the notion that heredity may contribute to heart disease, there may be important differences between lay and professional understandings of 'family' and of 'having a family history of heart disease'.

Hunt et al (2001) found differences within the Scottish population in terms of how people perceived the relationship between family history and risks of heart disease.

- Both people and doctors perceived the age at which relatives developed heart disease to be important.
- Both people and doctors perceived the closeness of the blood relationship to the relative to be an important indicator of risk.
- Notions of what constituted a 'premature' death varied in terms of both age and gender: deaths of working class men and women were considered the result of 'old age' rather than family history at younger ages, compared to middle class men and women who continued to attribute deaths to 'family history' at older ages.
- People with a large number of affected relatives did not necessarily transfer this into a perception of having a 'family history' of heart disease.
- People need to have some knowledge about patterns of illness and deaths in their family, but this information may be incomplete or missing, perhaps because of family arguments, geographical separation or because the key family member linking different sides of the family had died.
- People frequently made a distinction between family risk and personal risk. Whether individuals felt personally at greater risk depended upon the extent to which they felt they resembled particular family members or identified with particular sides of the family.

As Bhopal (2007) has argued, there is no simple unequivocal answer to the question of why coronary heart disease is so common among South Asians. The high rates are likely to arise from a combination of factors, and the control of the 'epidemic' of coronary heart disease requires a co-ordinated response. The National Service Framework on coronary heart disease makes special mention of the need to provide services that are accessible and acceptable to the people they serve. However, it is very important to develop strategies that recognise the heterogeneity of the South Asian population and acknowledge that risk factors vary considerably between communities. Disease registers and practice lists may need to have a valid ethnic code so that services can be targeted. Thresholds for action may need to be set lower for South Asians than the population as a whole. One illustration of this is body mass index. The World Health Organisation cut-off points for overweight and obesity were generated mostly in White populations. However, at any body mass index, on average, most Asian populations including the Chinese, Malays and South Asians have more fat than White populations, and so the cut-off point for these groups needs to be lower (Bhopal, 2007).

> ## GOOD PRACTICE: Coronary heart disease
>
> Project Dil: A co-ordinated primary care and community health promotion programme for reducing risk factors of coronary heart disease among the South Asian community of Leicester. This includes a coronary heart disease training and awareness programme for health care professionals; organisational change to ensure adoption of an effective secondary prevention programme for general practice and a public awareness campaign including a peer education programme for the South Asian community of Leicestershire.
>
> See: *Farooqi and Bhavsar (2001)*

Diabetes

As with heart disease, the incidence rate for diabetes is considerably raised in a number of minority ethnic groups compared to the general population (See *Figure 5.2*). However, again it is not ethnicity that causes the higher prevalence of diabetes.

South Asian patients with insulin-dependent diabetes suffer exceptionally high rates of mortality. Conversely, those born in China have lower or comparable rates to the general population (Sproston and Mindell, 2006).

As with heart disease, medical research has focused disproportionately on alleged genetic predispositions and on alleged 'cultural' diets. Again, we note the potential role that poverty, racism, and various sources of stress (lack of control at work, low place in a social hierarchy, lack of quality social support networks) may have in the genesis of higher rates of diabetes. Nevertheless, there is again an illness experience that cannot be reduced to a biological description of the disease, as indicated in the following two studies investigating lay beliefs about diabetes in the African-Caribbean and Bangladeshi communities, respectively.

African-Caribbean lay beliefs about diabetes

Pierce and Armstrong (1996) found differences even between two small focus groups of eight and nine African-Caribbean respondents. Not all those diagnosed with diabetes by a doctor had interpreted their condition as diabetes. Some said they had symptoms of diabetes but this was not regarded as the same as being diabetic. Others conceived themselves as having once had diabetes but not any longer as their weight was now under control.

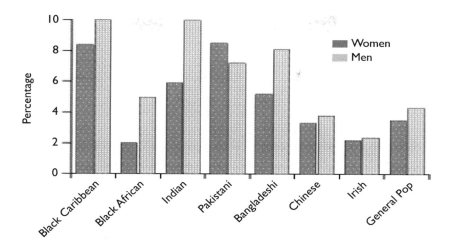

Figure 5.2. Prevalence of doctor-diagnosed diabetes within minority ethnic groups. From Health Survey for England (2004).

'Having sugar' and having diabetes were not necessarily regarded as the same thing. For some, diabetes was not a 'disease'. Rather, the category 'disease' was reserved for infectious or contagious conditions. By contrast diabetes was considered to be an 'ailment' or a 'situation'. Diabetes was represented as a problem of the control of sugar not of high sugar per se (perhaps because of the paradox that although the illness is linked to excess sugar, sugar was sometimes also the therapy required). Reference was made to the experiences of those working with sugar and having a high sugar intake back in the Caribbean who did not suffer the same problems as in the UK.

Weight gain was felt to be more to do with being 'born that way' and diet sheets were ridiculed because food (especially West Indian food) was considered an important resource for living, and changing eating patterns to improve life was therefore contradictory.

Some respondents expressed a belief that perspiration got rid of toxins of starchy foods, as if 'burned up' in the Caribbean sun and day-to-day priorities interfered with ideal treatment. People were not ignorant about incessant health education messages, but these medical lessons were embedded in much deeper cultural beliefs about health and illness.

Bangladeshi lay beliefs about diabetes

Kelleher and Islam's (1996) study found that, for the Bangladeshi community, food is important as an underpinning affirmation of social friendship. The refusal of food would be interpreted as withdrawal of friendship and exchange of food gives meaning around religious rituals. There is a belief that food is good for you and to deny food is unnatural. Rice is considered to be 'soul' food because it is a reminder of the homeland and it is part of the Bangladeshi identity as a 'rice-eating people' and has a ritual significance with children. Other beliefs included:

- Vegetables from above or under the ground were viewed differently (as for African-Caribbean people).
- Green, unripe, bitter fruit and vegetables were held to counteract the problem of sugar.
- Traditionally, being plump and well-fed were signs of wealth and health, although influences are now towards slimness.
- Eating Bangladeshi food was seen as part of retention of identity.
- Apart from karela (a bitter melon), for which there is some medical evidence, Bangladeshis do not think folk medicines or amulets are of use for diabetes.
- Most Bangladeshis fast in Ramadan and do not believe it affects their diabetes, although a minority believe it does, and do not fast because they believe there is a religious instruction that ill health is a reason to be excused fasting. Guidance to the management of diabetes in Ramadan is contained in Sheikh and Wallia (2007).

GOOD PRACTICE: Diabetes

Apnee Sehat (Our Health) South Warwickshire Primary Care Trust: This project was devised to support local South Asians in South Warwickshire to look at lifestyle changes to help prevent diabetes. The project involved working in partnership across traditional boundaries with the Primary Care Trust, University of Warwick, National Diabetes Support Team, Diabetes UK and local community leaders. The project produced a DVD featuring culturally acceptable tips on healthy living, ways of increasing exercise, and other health messages. The project also included cooking lessons at a local Gurdwara, including the production of low fat and low sugar sweets for Diwali celebrations and a Diwali health calendar

---

Hypertension

As with heart disease and diabetes, there is a dearth of medical research that examines the relationship between racism, internalised anger and high blood pressure. Once again, the lay construction of hypertension is a blend of medical models of disease and community experience. Interestingly epidemiological 'racialised' messages about African-Caribbeans exhibiting high rates of hypertension ('it's normal for African-Caribbeans') have been taken up in such a way as to make health education advice even less likely to be heeded.

Hypertension in African-Caribbean and White British people

Morgan (1996) interviewed both White and African-Caribbean people about hypertension.

- African-Caribbeans reported that they did not take their blood pressure medicines as prescribed, but that they had not told their doctors about this.
- African-Caribbeans derived comfort and reassurance from their relatives who had suffered strokes that their high blood pressure represented 'normality'.
- About half of both the White and the African-Caribbean groups interviewed did not know hypertension and high blood pressure were the same thing.
- African-Caribbeans understood hypertension to mean 'getting worked up/getting in a temper'.
- Tension, stress and worry were frequently cited causes of high blood pressure by both White and African-Caribbean respondents.

The significance of understanding lay explanations of hypertension has been confirmed in a more recent ethnographic study of the African-Caribbean community carried out by Higginbottom (2008).

Cancer

The belief that rates of cancer are relatively low in minority ethnic communities has begun to change. Latest estimates on the incidence of cancer among South Asians indicate that while older South Asians have low rates of cancer, the pattern among younger South Asians is changing with increased risks compared to non-South Asians. There is, however, little information relating to the incidence or prevalence of cancers among minority ethnic groups. Mortality from prostate and liver cancer is high among Black African and Caribbean groups, while the incidence of lung cancer is lower in all minority ethnic groups. Prostate cancer appears to progress more rapidly in Black than in White men. Breast cancer is lower in South Asian women and those born in the Caribbean, although it appears to be on the increase. Mortality from cancers of the oral cavity has been indicated to be five to 10 times higher in East African immigrants, compared to rates in England and Wales. The incidence of colorectal cancer in the South Asian population is significantly lower than in the general population. However, South Asian children have been shown to have an increased risk of lymphomas (both Hodgkins and non-Hodgkins) compared to White children. There is evidence of lower uptake of population cancer screening programmes, linked largely to poor knowledge, language barriers and administrative problems due to inaccurate addresses (Aspinall and Jacobson, 2004).

GOOD PRACTICE: Cancer

Westminster PCT has funded a Macmillan Cancer Information Drop-in Service for London Chinese communities. This aims to raise public awareness of cancer issues and provide cancer information and support sessions targeted at Chinese communities.

Cancer Black Care (www.cancerblackcare.org): This organisation, which serves the black and minority ethnic (BME) community, has centres in Lambeth, Birmingham and Manchester that provide practical, physical and emotional support for people with all types of cancer and their families, relatives and friends. They provide culturally appropriate and relevant information on all aspects of cancer care. A drop-in service is available plus a telephone helpline and advocacy service. One-to-one counselling is offered by trained counsellors. Twi, Yoruba, Hindi, Turkish and other languages are spoken. Advice on general welfare benefits and grants, prevention, screening, palliative care and supportive care are available. The organisation also runs a volunteer befriending scheme that provides home/hospital visiting.

Sickle cell and thalassaemia

Sickle cell and the thalassaemias are serious inherited haemoglobin disorders. Because there is a well-known Mendelian pattern of inheritance, and there is an association between rates of carrying genes associated with sickle cell or thalassaemia and different populations, the conditions are sometimes wrongly taken as evidence that there is at least some basis for the claim that there really are distinct 'races'. There is a correlation between some socially constructed ethnic categories and the incidence of carrying genes associated with sickle cell or thalassaemia. The genes are found more frequently in peoples of African, Mediterranean, Middle Eastern, South Asian and South-East Asian descent. However, genes associated with invisible haemoglobin variants, and genes associated with somatic features such as skin colour, are inherited separately. The genes associated with sickle cell and thalassaemia are found to some extent in all populations, and the current statistical association with particular socially defined ethnic categories will decrease over time. It is for reasons such as these that in England the NHS Sickle Cell and Thalassaemia Screening Programme has examined the problems of using ethnicity as a screening question to help target screening programmes towards those statistically at higher risk.

At the time of writing, the screening policies in England are as follows:

- Neonatal screening: all new-born infants (irrespective of ethnicity) are offered screening for sickle cell by means of the Guthrie blood spot test. This will identify those with a form of sickle cell disease so that treatment can begin, including prophylactic penicillin, flu vaccinations, and education of parents on signs of a sickle cell crisis, including advice on how to palpate the spleen. The programme will also identify sickle cell carriers (sickle cell trait).
- Antenatal screening: in some areas where there are high proportions of people recorded in high risk groups, universal antenatal screening is offered. The laboratory screening tests begin to identify those who may have be carriers of alpha or beta-thalassaemia (the first stage is an assessment of red blood cell indices as part of the full blood count) and those who may be carriers of sickle cell or another clinically relevant variant haemoglobin (such as haemoglobin C, D-Punjab, or O-Arab). In other low prevalence areas, initial screening is by means of a family origins question, specifically designed by the NHS Sickle Cell and Thalassaemia Screening Programme. This identifies those parents who, on the basis of their self-assignment to socially constructed ethnic categories, are statistically more likely to carry genes associated with sickle cell or thalassaemia. These mothers (and where the mother is a carrier, also the father) are offered the laboratory screening tests. It is likely that, in the future, healthcare providers may be encouraged to offer a haemoglobinopathy screen to all new patients joining the practice, as currently antenatal screening for sickle cell and thalassaemia sometimes occurs too late to allow couples the option of discontinuing a pregnancy (Dormandy et al, 2008). Although these inherited disorders are extremely important to the families

who experience the full disorders, it is also important to bear in mind that morbidity and mortality associated with haemoglobin disorders makes only a slight contribution to the overall patterns of health of minority ethnic groups in the UK, for whom differential rates of heart disease, diabetes and hypertension are much larger contributory factors to overall population health.

GOOD PRACTICE: Sickle cell/thalassaemia screening

In general practice the window of opportunity is small, as many mothers do not present for confirmation of pregnancy until after their second missed period. Even with early electrophoresis, if the woman is found to be a carrier it is necessary then to find her partner and persuade him to come for testing. To overcome these time constraints, one practice offers all men and women haemoglobinopathy screening based on their self-perception of risk. Screening is undertaken at a registration check and opportunistically within the practice, with counselling both before and after the test. This service is acceptable to patients, with high uptake in appropriate ethnic groups and a high attendance at follow up visits, when they are given results and a haemoglobinopathy card. The results are readily available on the computer screen and in the general practice record. Any patients found to carry a significant trait are advised to present early for antenatal care should they or their partner become pregnant. Pre-conception haemoglobinopathy testing removes some of the additional anxiety for the patient in early pregnancy by identifying risk earlier and allows more time to organise prenatal diagnosis should it be necessary. (From Logan, 2000: 1542.)

As the NHS Screening Programme progresses GPs may need to ensure continued professional development for their practice nurses. For example, one way of managing neonatal screening information that an infant is a sickle cell carrier is to flag this up in the medical record for the practice nurse to undertake some health education at the time the child reaches puberty.

Further information is available from Dyson (2005) or by visiting http://www.chime.ucl.ac.uk/APoGI/

Hepatitis B and C

There are important ethnic variations in the prevalence and modes of transmission of hepatitis B and C. This provides an excellent illustration of the need to understand the significance of ethnicity in relation to health and healthcare. While around 80% of hepatitis C (HCV) infections in the White population are thought to occur in injecting drug users, in minority ethnic communities there is a different pattern of infection. There is emerging evidence of high prevalence rates in the UK Pakistani community. In Pakistan high rates of HCV (up to 20% of the population in some areas) are thought to be related to unsafe medical and dental treatment (unsterile therapeutic injections, blood transfusions), or other high-risk activities such as barber shop/street shaving using cut-throat razors. Members of the UK community who regularly visit Pakistan need to be informed of the potential dangers of these practices. While there is no vaccination for HCV, there is an effective treatment and screening of some minority ethnic groups should be considered. Deaths from hepatocellular carcinoma with any mention of hepatitis C are continuing to rise in the UK.

There is also a higher prevalence of hepatitis B (HBV) in several minority ethnic communities. HBV is much more infectious than HVC. Chronic HBV infection is more common in Africa and Asia, parts of the Middle East and some eastern European countries. One study (Kawsar and Goh, 2002) estimated that up to 50% of the population of Hong Kong may have been exposed to HBV. This is acquired predominantly in childhood, either by perinatal transmission from an infected mother or by horizontal transmission between young children. In the White UK population most infections are acquired in adulthood, where sexual transmission and injecting drug use account for a significant proportion of new infections. When acquired at an early age, infection is much more likely to become chronic and to be asymptomatic. A safe and effective vaccine is available and should be considered for some groups. High rates of hepatitis infection and death due to hepatitis-related end-stage liver disease are found in North African and South-East Asian groups.

The potential impact of diagnosing these two infections is important and while screening of the entire UK population is thought unlikely to be a cost-effective option, improving case finding in minority ethnic communities originating from countries where these infections are common is likely to be of major benefit. Again, healthcare practices may consider immunisation and certainly health information for patients travelling to countries of origin, where they may undertake cultural practices and medical treatment which place them at increased risk of infection.

For information on hepatitis see publications from the British Liver Trust (www.britishlivertrust.org.uk) the Hepatitis B Foundation (www.hepb.org. uk) and the Hepatitis C Trust (www.hepctrust.org.uk).

Making sense of illness

In this chapter, we have considered some of the common issues that may affect clients of minority ethnic descent in the UK. However, it should be noted that these brief sketches of lay understandings can do little more than attune us to the potential sources of influence on health behaviours. It is clear that for all groups, White British Christian people included, it is never simply a matter of 'having' a clear-cut, medically defined specific disease. All patients are active in making sense of their illness, for which they may draw upon lay health beliefs, alternative sources of healing, and different aspects of the medical model of the disease and its treatment.

The blending of ideas from different belief systems is an achievement of the patient that may be carried out in different ways depending upon the particular context. The word achievement is important in this respect. The professional–client encounter is one that is usually characterised as a technical expert and a lay non-expert, possibly beset by a series of misconceptions. However, note how clients have to be very skilled indeed in assessing their own signs and symptoms and deciding whether or not to consult a doctor. They have to recognise something is amiss; consult family members and friends; assess the impact of what is troubling them on their work and/ or family commitments; make decisions about self-medication with home remedies, over-the-counter medicines or alternative treatments; and situate their experience in relation to a religious world-view. Having executed this series of skilful decisions, and decided to consult a doctor, different patients may slip into a passive deferential and self-effacing patient role readily, reluctantly, partially or not at all. How they achieve this transformation, and the extent to which they achieve it, is likely to vary within as well as between different ethnic groups.

Medication

In prescribing any medication it is necessary to consider the factors that may affect peoples' willingness or ability to comply. Most people will comply with advice and treatment that they understand and that seem sensible to them, and they are less likely to stop taking medicine if possible side effects have been explained to them. There may, however, be cultural and religious issues which need to be considered in this process. People less familiar with Western medication may believe that Western drugs are 'too strong' for them; people for whom hair loss has special religious significance may cease taking medication if hair loss is experienced; and people who observe strict codes of cleanliness and modesty may be especially distressed at side effects such as incontinence or diarrhoea.

Specific advice should be given to Muslim patients who may be fasting during Ramadan. Although the sick and infirm are not obliged to fast and ongoing medication is exempt, some Muslim patients will wish to fast whatever the circumstances. Fasting patients will not take medication by mouth, nose or suppository between dawn and sunset, although some may accept injections or intravenous infusions. It is helpful to find out the exact dates for Ramadan each year (available from www.diversiton.com/religion/) so that appropriate care and advice can be given and possible problems discussed. It may be possible to adjust medication to fit in with the fast, e.g. using slow-release preparations, or prescribing tablets to be taken twice a day. Discussion with each patient about whether and how they plan to keep the fast, and what they are likely to eat and drink and when, can help prevent major problems due to non-compliance.

There are also cultural differences in the methods of administration of medication with which people feel comfortable (the French for example, receive many drugs by suppository). In many developing countries injections are thought to be particularly effective.

Drugs containing ingredients derived from pork are not acceptable to many Muslims and Jewish people. However, within each faith there are many different schools of thought; the intensity of religious observance will vary between individuals and faith-based judgements may exempt such medicines in certain circumstances. In Judaism for example, porcine-derived medication is only an issue with oral medication and even then only if the medication is regarded as 'edible'. The best way to approach this problem is to involve patients in decisions about their medication. A list of common drugs of porcine origin and their alternatives are discussed in a booklet published by the Medicine Partnership in association with the Muslim Council of Great Britain (2004).

Key points

- We need to avoid 'racialising' differences in patterns of major diseases such as heart disease, diabetes and hypertension associated with different ethnic groups. There is often an explanation linked to:
  - level of material deprivation
  - level of stress caused by place in a social hierarchy
  - level of stress linked to degree of control over one's work
  - extent to which stress is mitigated by differing levels of social support.
- Heart disease offers some specific challenges for community health professionals. Patients need to recognise the effects of smoking, diet and exercise on health. Healthcare providers need to recognise the effects of social factors, which may be beyond the immediate control of either providers or patients. Patients may have different understandings of the concept of a 'family history of heart disease'.
- For diseases such as heart disease, diabetes, hypertension and cancer, patients may blend their lay apprehending of technical medical knowledge with social, historical and cultural beliefs to create a complex view of the illness experience.
- There is evidence of a lower uptake of population cancer screening programmes among some minority groups.
- Hepatitis B and C appear to be more common in some minority ethnic groups. It may be appropriate to consider case finding for HCV in UK subjects who were born in the Indian sub-continent, especially Pakistan where prevalence is high. Vaccination for and health information about HBV should be considered for some minority ethnic groups.
- There are cultural and religious differences in approaches to medication which should be discussed with patients.

References

Aspinall PJ, Jacobson B (2004) *Ethnic Disparities in Health and Health Care*. Department of Health, London

Bhopal R (2007) *Ethnicity, Race and Health in Multicultural Societies*. Oxford University Press, Oxford

Dormandy E, Gulliford MC, Reid EP, Brown K, Marteau T (2008) Delay between pregnancy confirmation and sickle cell and thalassaemia screening: A population-based cohort study. *British Journal of General Practice* 58: 154–9

Dyson SM (2005) *Ethnicity and Screening for Sickle Cell and Thalassaemia*. Elsevier Churchill Livingstone, Oxford

Farooqi A, Bhavsar M (2001) Project Dil: A co-ordinated Primary Care and Community Health Promotion Programme for reducing risk factors of coronary heart disease amongst the South Asian community of Leicester – experiences and evaluation of the project. *Ethnicity and Health* **6**(3–4): 265–70

Higginbottom G (2008) "I didn't tell them. Well, they never ask". Lay understandings of hypertension and their impact on chronic disease management: Implications for nursing practice in primary care. *Journal of Research in Nursing* **13**: 89–99

Hunt K, Emslie C, Watt G (2001) Lay constructions of a family history of heart disease: Potential for misunderstandings in the clinical encounter. *The Lancet* **357**(9263): 1168–71

Kawsar M, Goh B (2002) Hepatitis B virus infection among Chinese residents in the United Kingdom. *Sexually Transmitted Infections* **78**: 166–8

Kelleher D, Islam S (1996) 'How should I live?' Bangladeshi people and non-insulin-dependent diabetes. In Kelleher D, Hillier S (eds) *Researching Cultural Differences in Health* (pp 220–37). Routledge, London

Logan J (2000) Haemoglobinopathy screening can be carried out in general practice. *British Medical Journal* **320**: 1542

Medicine Partnership in association with the Muslim Council of Great Britain (2004) *Drugs of Porcine Origin and Clinical Alternatives*. Available from: www.mcb.org.uk/uploads/PBEnglish.pdf [last accessed 20 August 2009]

Morgan M (1996) The meanings of high blood pressure among Afro-Caribbean and white patients. In Kelleher D, Hillier S (eds) *Researching Cultural Differences in Health* (pp 11–37). Routledge, London

Pierce M, Armstrong D (1996) Afro-Caribbean lay beliefs about diabetes: An exploratory study. In Kelleher D, Hillier S (eds) *Researching Cultural Differences in Health* (pp 91–102). Routledge, London

Rodmell S, Watt A (eds) (1986) *The Politics of Health Education*. Routledge and Kegan Paul, London

Sheikh A, Wallia S (2007) Ramadan fasting and diabetes. *British Medical Journal* **335**: 613–4

Sproston K, Mindell J (2006) *Health Survey for England 2004: The Health of Ethnic Minority Groups*. The Stationery Office, London

Wilkinson RG (1996) *Unhealthy Societies: The Afflictions of Inequality*. Routledge, London

Further reading

British Heart Foundation (2004) *Heart Disease and South Asians*. Department of Health, London

Bhui K, Warfa N, Edonya P, McKenzie K, Bhugra D (2007) Cultural competence in mental health care: A review of model evaluations. *BMC Health Services Research* **7**: 15. doi:10.1186/1472-6963-7-15

Saxena Sm Misra T, Car J, Netuveli G, Smith R, Majeed A (2007) Systematic Review of Primary Healthcare Interventions to Improve Diabetes Outcomes in Minority Ethnic Groups. *Journal of Ambulatory Care Management* **30**(3): 218–30

Sproston K, Mindell J (2006) *Health Survey for England 2004: The Health of Ethnic Minority Groups*. The Stationery Office, London (This survey focuses on the health of minority ethnic groups using a sample of participants from Black Caribbean, Indian, Pakistani, Bangladeshi, Chinese and Irish communities. Results of the survey are compared with the general population in England. This survey covers self-reported health and psychosocial wellbeing; cardiovascular disease; diabetes; smoking and use of tobacco; drinking; anthropometric measures; overweight, and obesity; physical activity; blood pressure; eating habits; blood analysis; use of complementary medicine; children's health.)

CHAPTER 6

Disease in context: family and community

In this chapter, we look at the ongoing management of acute and chronic disease in the community. Clearly most patients are part of broader family and community networks within which they make sense of their health. However, there are popular misconceptions about the nature of family and extended kinship networks in relation to minority ethnic groups in the UK. We also examine other community influences on health, such as traditional healers (Chinese herbalists, acupuncturists, ayurvedic healers and hakims from the Unani system of medicine), and ask if such practices differ greatly from how White patients use complementary medicine and 'Western' medicine flexibly and contingently.

Some misconceptions about family and kin in minority ethnic groups include the following:

- The notion that community care services are less needed for British Asian families, with the stereotyped assumption that they can be expected to 'look after their own'. This has been widely criticised.
- Different groups may attach different meanings and values to the key concept of independence. Dependency may be understood as a sense of mutual obligation and reciprocal care. As such, becoming independent may not have the positive connotations for some that it may have for health professionals.
- Not all groups would accept stereotypical views of caring for disabled people, or themselves living with disablement, as a 'burden'. Not least, such stereotypes ignore the care given by those who may also be cared for.
- Some informal caring may be made possible by forms of disadvantage, i.e. lack of opportunity for paid employment because of discrimination in educational opportunity and in the labour market. This may increase the availability of people to undertake unpaid caring.

As can be seen from *Table 6.1*, households from minority ethnic groups are more likely to have dependent children than are White families. However, it would be a mistake to assume that larger families are part of the 'culture' of different ethnic groups, for several reasons:

- Minority ethnic groups have a younger age structure than the ageing White population. Statistically, they are more likely to be of child-rearing age.
- There is a strong association between families on lower incomes and greater number of children. Families from minority ethnic backgrounds are statistically over-represented in more poorly paid occupations, and their greater number of children is partly an effect of this concentration in less affluent households. This can be seen in the way in which the British Asian ethnic group that has become most affluent (Indian) has a lower proportion of families with children compared to Pakistani and Bangladeshi populations.
- Globally, larger families are associated with a lack of alternative societal entitlements to care in older age or disablement. Certainly migrant generations may not have built up welfare benefit rights or pension rights based on length of working life in the UK, and to that extent preference for children may also be an artefact of socio-economic position, as well as a 'cultural imperative'.

The composition of White families, with only around two-fifths having dependent children, reflects different age structures within different ethnic groups (see *Table 6.2*). The White population has a larger proportion of single

Table 6.1. Families with dependent children as a proportion of all families by ethnic group. April 2001, UK

White	42%
Mixed	65%
Indian	58%
Pakistani	72%
Bangladeshi	79%
Other Asian	64%
Black Caribbean	62%
Black African	75%
Black other	75%
Chinese	57%
Other ethnic group	64%

From: Office for National Statistics: UK Census 2001. www.statistics.gov.uk
Reproduced with the permission of the Controller of HMSO

and lone pensioner households compared to other ethnic groups. By contrast the younger age structures of the Bangladeshi, Pakistani, Black African and 'Black other' communities leads to a situation with over 70% of these families have dependent children, and nearly 80% for the Bangladeshi community.

In addition to having greater proportions of families with dependent children, some of the minority ethnic groups also have larger families, with 40% of Pakistani and Bangladeshi families with dependent children having three or more children at the 2001 Census. The comparable figures for Whites was 17%, with Black African 28%, and Indian families 20%.

Over three-quarters of the UK families of Indian, Pakistani, Bangladeshi and Chinese descent with dependent children were in married households, and in the case of British Asian (Indians) the figure was 85%.

Co-habitation was more common among White, mixed and Black Caribbean couples, at around 12% each, but was less common, although still forming a small part of the overall picture, for British South Asians, Chinese and Black Africans.

All ethnic groups have at least one in eight families led by a lone parent, including the British South Asians, with nearly one in five Pakistani families headed by a lone parent. The highest proportions of families with dependent children were in the mixed, Black Caribbean, and Black (other) categories, with the rate for Whites in between at around 25%.

Table 6.2. Families with dependent children: by ethnic group and family type. April 2001, UK

	Married couple	Co-habiting couple	Lone parent
White	63%	12%	25%
Mixed	42%	12%	64%
Indian	85%	2%	13%
Pakistani	78%	3%	19%
Bangladeshi	79%	3%	18%
Other Asian	81%	3%	16%
Black Caribbean	30%	12%	58%
Black African	44%	5%	51%
Black other	26%	10%	64%
Chinese	79%	3%	18%
Other ethnic group	73%	4%	23%

From: Office for National Statistics: UK Census 2001. www.statistics.gov.uk
Reproduced with the permission of the Controller of HMSO

A model for thinking about family may be to think of how social, economic, political and cultural circumstances may change the nature of the relationship between wider society and the individual.

Kinship obligations

Since the 1990s an increasing number of reports have identified a widespread assumption on the part of health and social care service providers that people of South Asian descent 'look after their own' (Walker and Ahmad, 1994); that is they automatically enjoy a cohesive and extended family network of support as part of their alleged cultural attributes. However, this has been shown to be a misplaced assumption (Katbamna et al, 2004), not least because statistically, South Asian households are more likely to conform to stereotypical 'norms' of a nuclear household, with two parents and children, than are either White British or African-Caribbean households. Instead some commentators (Katbamna et al, 2004) have suggested that myths of 'looking after one's own' have functioned as an excuse neither to investigate nor put right the lack of access to health and social care services for minority ethnic groups.

Below, we see how the concept of *biraderi* among people of Pakistani Muslim descent, plays out in a complex way that bears little direct relation to its idealised form.

The issue at stake for the care of patients is not what cultural beliefs they hold, but what practical, emotional, social and financial support they can expect from which significant others, and what obligations to care do they themselves fulfil to others.

Biraderi and kinship obligations

A *biraderi* is, in its narrowest sense, a network of blood relatives from both the mother's and father's side of the family, who all share obligations (*duniyadari*) to one another for moral, social and financial support. This network is governed by reciprocal giving of gifts, often associated with key life cycle events such as birth, marriage and death, or with other special religious occasions. The different *biraderi* are ranked within a broader hierarchy, *zat*, associated with kinship, occupation passed down from kin, land ownership, area of origin and political alliances. However:

- *Zat* is itself ostensibly at odds with the egalitarianism claimed for Islam
- *Biraderi* can be used more broadly to encompass those from the same area of origin even though they are from a different *zat*.
- *Biraderi* can be used in a still broader sense to include all Muslim and/ or Pakistani neighbours who are not kin.

- *Biraderi* can be used in its very broadest sense of all to include all non-Muslim Asian and White neighbours, where it is perceived that there is a common bond of shared territory and political concerns.

As we move from the more restricted meaning of *biraderi* to the broader ones, the moral imperatives associated with incremental gift-giving are correspondingly reduced.

Numbers and degree of concentration make a difference to if and how a *biraderi* works in practice. In inner city areas, geographical space and kin networks may almost be co-terminous.

Life experience may help define *biraderi*, as in the case of a Mirpuri family not supported by their relatives, but who were given practical help instead by their Pathan and Gujarati-Hindu neighbours. Life experience might also lead someone to view the *biraderi* concept as a myth, as one Pathan disabled mother found when abandoned by her husband and kin. Younger generations are less familiar with the concept of *biraderi* and may mistakenly equate it with notions of caste.

Some of the more affluent middle-class Pakistani Muslims regard *biraderi* as an almost negative mark of distinction that defines 'others' as uneducated, rural and backward-looking in contrast to self-perceptions of themselves as urban, upper class and educated. On the other hand idealised versions of *biraderi*, emphasising an idealised past, a connection to a past homeland, and a sense of moral superiority, may be drawn upon to distinguish between Pakistani (or even all South Asian) families compared to 'Whites' who were constructed as different (Chattoo et al, 2004).

Consanguinity

A particular area that has concerned health professionals, especially around community genetics, is the issue of consanguinity, or marriage to a first cousin.

As can be seen below it would be very easy, but inaccurate and unhelpful, to blame either consanguinity or those communities practising consanguinity, for the presence of genetic disorders, and indeed clusters of genetic disorders should make the provision of good community genetics services easier to provide. According to Ahmad (1994), Ahmed et al (2002) and Darr (1990, 2005):

- Studies alleging birth defects are often poorly controlled for level of material deprivation, which is itself associated with increased levels of birth defects.
- Not all British Pakistani Muslim groups practice this form of marriage.

- Consanguinity is practised across the world. Twenty per cent of the human population live in communities with a preference for consanguineous marriage and 8.5% of all global births are to consanguineous parents.
- It is wrong to equate consanguineous marriage with a lifestyle choice: it is a complex decision based on assessment of likely levels of social support, socio-economic circumstances, experience of racism or hostility from wider society.
- Marriage between two individuals who are cousins, in itself, is not the cause of recessive conditions such as beta-thalassaemia major. Blaming consanguinity for the birth of affected children is both inaccurate and unhelpful.
- Health education messages can be disbelieved because people witness cousin marriages without disabled children, and also see disabled children born to non-consanguineous parents.
- Epidemiological findings show that manifestations of recessive conditions occur as clusters within communities with a preference for consanguineous marriage, rather than sporadically throughout the population. This greatly simplifies the process of identifying clusters of carriers of recessive variant genes in these communities.
- The required response is for carrier detection plus adequate genetic counselling facilities that allow people to make informed choices, based on accurate information about their individual risk; available data show that information and support to at-risk British Pakistani families is grossly deficient.
- The practice of consanguinity can reduce stigma against disabled people as it is less likely that people will stigmatise those they consider to be part of their own family network.

Complementary, alternative and traditional therapies

The various complementary and traditional therapies are an important part of the patient's potential armamentarium, irrespective of ethnic group. As was suggested in *Chapter 1*, all patients potentially consult a network of people before going to see the medical doctor. Such people may be family, friends, work colleagues and neighbours, or they may be other members of the formal healthcare system such as pharmacists or community nurses. The network may comprise lay healers, alternative therapists and traditional practitioners operating within different medical systems. In some cases 'alternative' practitioners may be a misnomer since the person may be dual qualified in more than one system of healing. The network may also include those from whom health guidance is set within a broader spiritual context, such as clergy, priests or imams.

Earlier we suggested that an appropriate ethos of healthcare practice in a multi-ethnic society would be to make links with the range of traditional practitioners in the area served. Alternative therapies have potential adverse outcomes, just as Western medicine sometimes has. However, even if a doctor regards some alternative therapies as harmful, an outright antagonism is likely to be counter-productive. If there is a three-way communication between healthcare provider, traditional practitioner, and patient, the health professional is more likely to be able to challenge and question the practices than if they are 'underground'; and is more likely also to distinguish between those practitioners formally accredited and those who may not be.

Even if the health professional were to judge the alternative treatments as ineffective but not in themselves harmful, it would still be important to engage with traditional healers. Since patients may consult both traditional and Western healthcare providers, it makes sense to encourage them to share knowledge about what other treatments they are receiving, not least to avoid the harm of interactions between pharmaceutical drugs and alternative therapies (see *Table 6.3*).

Finally, if the treatments and advice are regarded by the health professional as beneficial, then maintaining a good network, within which traditional and medical healthcare providers can negotiate treatment with their patients, may be of mutual benefit to patient, provider and traditional practitioner. In short, such links could become part of the repertoire of medical practice.

Some traditional healing systems

- *Acupuncture* is a form of traditional Chinese medicine which consists of the insertion and manipulation of special needles into key acupuncture points of the body.
- *Ayurveda* is an ancient Indian medical system or, in Sanskrit, the science of life. The basis for health is a balance between elements, which occur in three combinations, or tridoshas: Vatha (relating to the nervous system and the body's centre of energy); Pitta (metabolism, enzymes, acid and bile); and Kapha (mucous membranes, phlegm, fat and lymph system). Three-point diagnosis involves observation, examination by touch and detailed life and health history. Treatment is specific to the individual and the practitioner, but may involve diet, purification, herbalism, meditation, massage, breathing and exercise.
- Herbalism is part of traditional Chinese medicine. Herbs may be of a 'hot' or 'cold' nature. They be may be sweet, sour, bitter, salty or pungent in taste. They may act on different channels within the body.
- Unani originated in Greece, and was developed by Arabic and Persian scholars and practised in India. It has similiarities to ayurveda in aiming

Table 6.3. Important potential interactions between herbal preparations and conventional drugs

Herb	Conventional drug	Potential problem
Echinacea used for >8 weeks	Anabolic steroids, methotrexate, amiodarone, ketoconazole	Hepatotoxicity
Feverfew	Non-steroidal anti-inflammatory drugs	Inhibition of herbal effect
Feverfew, garlic, ginseng, gingko, ginger	Warfarin	Altered bleeding time
Ginseng	Phenelzine sulphate	Headache, tremulousness, manic episodes
Ginseng	Oestrogens, corticosteroids	Additive effects
St John's wort	Monoamine oxidase inhibitor and serotonin reuptake inhibitor antidepressants	Mechanism of herbal effect uncertain. Insufficient evidence of safety with concomitant use, therefore not advised
St John's wort, saw palmetto	Iron	Tannic acid content of herbs may limit iron absorption
Valerian	Barbiturates	Additive effects, excessive sedation
Kyushin, liquorice, plantain, uzara root, hawthorn, ginseng	Digoxin	Interference with pharmacodynamics and drug level monitoring
Evening primrose oil, borage	Anticonvulsants	Lowered seizure threshold
Shankapulshpi (ayurvedic preparation)	Phenytoin	Reduced drug levels, inhibition of drug effect
Kava	Benzodiazepines	Additive sedative effects, coma
Echinacea, zinc (immunostimulants)	Immunosuppressants (such as corticosteroids, cyclosporin)	Antagonistic effects
Kelp	Thyroxine	Iodine content of herb may interfere with thyroid replacement
Liquorice	Spironolactone	Antagonism of diuretic effect
Karela, ginseng	Insulin, sulphonylureas, biguanides	Altered glucose concentrations. Should not be prescribed in diabetic patients

Source: Miller (1998)

to restore the balance of different bodily humours, each with its own temperament in terms of the binary oppositions hot–cold and wet–dry.

- Siddah is a system originating in Tamil Nadu (south India) with similarities to ayurveda, being based on restoration of the essential elements of the body.

- Traditional African healing encompasses a huge variety of traditions. Some healers will be knowledgeable about potential benefits of specific herbs, tree barks, and plants. Others may be involved in a belief system around spiritualism, in which, because the healer has links to ancestors, the healer has access to information and can share this with those who seek assistance, help and care. Asking questions as to whether the individuals treated have enemies or rivals over a particular issue, or if they desire something that is currently unfulfilled, helps direct the healers to support people's emotional health and their place in the normative network of the particular society.

- Traditional Chinese medicine conceives of illness as the consequence of an imbalance of the vital life energy Ch'i (or Qi). Ill health is held to result from an imbalance between the opposite and interdependent forces of Yin and Yang. The network of channels in which such forces may stagnate are called meridians.

Palliative care

Several studies have demonstrated low levels of knowledge about and access to palliative care services (Gunaratnam, 2007). People from minority ethnic groups are less likely to know others who have been in a hospice or received help from Macmillan or Marie Curie support workers or to ask their GPs for access to such services. There is less evidence that access problems relate to cultural or religious traditions (such as a desire 'to look after our own') than to low levels of cancer knowledge, lack of awareness of services available and their cultural appropriateness. Poor communication has been identified in several studies as a major barrier to uptake of palliative care by

---

GOOD PRACTICE: Palliative care

The National Council for Hospice and Specialist Palliative Care Services has produced a 12-minute video on palliative care in Cantonese, Gujarati, Hindi, Punjabi and Urdu. It is available from: www.hospice-spc-council.org.uk

A South Asian Palliative Care Awareness Arts Project in Birmingham has produced a 30-minute video on palliative care in Hindi. Tel: 0121 627 2469/2531

ethnic minorities. Recommendations made by researchers include improved interpreting services and appropriate literature; more systematic referral arrangements with general practitioners and improved ethnic monitoring in palliative care.

Key points

- Forms of family household composition are varied both between and within different ethnic groups.
- We need to establish the care-giving obligations and the potential to receive practical care in the case of each individual patient, rather than make stereotypical assumptions about health and social care needs based on the likely forms of extended family available.
- Particular forms of kinship networks such as *biraderi* and consanguinity are not in themselves guarantees of care patterns nor the cause of genetic conditions. They exist in interaction with wider societal experiences, including poverty and racism, and in practice may play out in complex and even contradictory ways.
- Clients from all ethnic groups have a network of significant others available to them, including alternative and traditional practitioners. Negotiating care in a three-way communication between health professional, patient and practitioner is likely to be more productive than an antagonistic stance.

References

Ahmad W (1994) Reflections on the consanguinity and birth outcome debate. *Journal of Public Health Medicine* **16**(4): 423–8

Ahmed S, Bekker H, Hewison J, Kinsey S (2002) Thalassaemia carrier testing in Pakistani adults: Behaviour, knowledge and attitudes. *Community Genetics* **5**(2): 120–7

Chattoo S, Atkin K, McNeish D (2004) *Young People of Pakistani Origins and Their Families: Implications for Providing Support to Young People and Their Families.* Family Services Support Leeds: Centre for Research in Primary Care/Barnardos Lottery Fund Project URN:RB217591. Available from: http://www.barnardos.org.uk/finalreport.pdf [accessed 14 June 2006]

Darr A (1990) *The Social Implications of Thalassaemia Among Muslims of Pakistani Origin in England: Family Experience and Service Delivery.* PhD Thesis University of London.

Darr A (2005) Consanguineous marriage in context: Delivering equitable services. *Bio News* 337

Gunaratnam Y (2007) *Improving the Quality of Palliative Care.* Race Equality Foundation, London

Katbamna S, Ahmad W, Bhakta P, Baker R, Parker G (2004) Do they look after their own?

Informal support for South Asian carers. *Health and Social Care in the Community* **12**(5): 398–406

Miller LG (1998) Herbal medicinals: Selected clinical considerations focusing on known or potential drug-herb interactions. *Archives of Internal Medicine* **158**: 2200–11

Walker R, Ahmad WIU (1994) Windows of opportunity in rotting frames: Care providers' perspectives on community care and black communities. *Critical Social Policy* **40**: 46–68

Further reading

Ahmad WIU (ed) (2000) *Ethnicity, Disability and Chronic Illness*. Open University Press, Buckingham

Jack C, Penny E, Nazar W (2001) Effective palliative care for minority ethnic groups: The role of a liaison worker. *International Journal of Palliative Nursing* **7**(8): 375–80

Modood T, Berhoud R, Lakey J, Nazroo J, Smith P, Virdee S, Beishon S (1997) *Ethnic Minorities in Britain: Diversity and Disadvantage*. Fourth National Survey of Ethnic Minorities. Policy Studies Institute, London

CHAPTER 7

Mental health and substance use

In this chapter, we examine issues concerning mental health, psychological problems and use of substances. A good deal of the challenge of working on mental health issues is that the Western notion of a sharp distinction between mind and body is not a spilt that characterises many other world views. This makes the relationship between ethnicity and mental health one that is particularly controversial. The issue of 'racialisation' (see *Chapter 1*) also applies to mental health status. Racialisation is the process by which characteristics deriving from circumstances that are specific to socio-economic and status position in society are inappropriately treated as if they were essential core genetic and/or cultural characteristics of an ethnic group. This also applies to the issue of substance misuse, where an additional challenge is to avoid linking specific, perhaps exotic, drugs with particular ethnic groups and at the same time to recognise that minority numbers within ethnic minority groups may have problems with use of substances that, at an epidemiological level, are not highly associated with that group.

Problems of mental health

There are several overlapping issues at stake when considering the mental health of patients from minority ethnic groups, including differences in causation of mental health problems, issues of comparability of the meanings of behaviours across cultures, and the impact of wider contexts such as material deprivation and experience of racism on mental health.

The work of James Nazroo (see Nazroo, 1997) suggests that a major problem is the racialisation of the issue of mental health. British-born minorities appear to have worse mental health than those who have migrated to the UK. This suggests that migration is a poor explanation for much of the difference in mental health. Furthermore, migrants, in turn, have worse mental health than their equivalents in the countries of origin who have not migrated. This implies that both genetics and 'cultural difference' are very weak explanations of these patterns. If migration, genetics and 'culture' are not good explanations, we need to look elsewhere. We need to look at the experience of racism; the patterning of mental health in relation to levels of material deprivation (there is a strong inverse relationship between rates of reported mental illness and level of deprivation within all ethnic groups); and the working practices of health professionals.

Evidence on ethnicity and mental health

It is commonly accepted that mental health problems can result from the range of adverse socio-economic factors associated with disadvantage and discrimination and these can also be a cause of social exclusion. Nowhere is this more evident than amongst black and minority ethnic groups. The extent of social exclusion among these communities, the levels of racism and racial discrimination experienced by them in public life and, more pertinently, when they come into contact with institutional agencies are key determinants of psychiatric morbidity within black and minority ethnic groups.

(Sashidharan, 2003)

Large-scale community surveys of ethnicity and psychiatric conditions which provide the most comprehensive data on the ethnic patterning of mental health (The EMPIRIC study, Sprotson and Nazroo 2000) have found only small ethnic differences in the prevalence of common mental disorders. There is evidence of ethnic differences in risk factors that operate before a patient comes into contact with health services (e.g. discrimination, social exclusion) and there is evidence of differences in treatment. It is likely that some mental health problems in people from minority groups go unreported because of the reluctance of people from those groups to engage with traditional healthcare services. It is also likely that some forms of mental health problems are over-reported in people whose first language is not English.

Irish people living in the United Kingdom have much higher hospital admission rates for mental health problems (depression and alcohol problems) compared with other ethnic groups and they are more likely to commit suicide. Despite these high rates, the campaigning group Mind argues that the needs of Irish people are often not taken into account in planning and delivering mental health services. African-Caribbean people have lower rates of minor psychiatric disorders than other ethnic groups but are more likely to be given a diagnosis of severe mental illness (three to five times more likely to be diagnosed and admitted to hospital for schizophrenia than any other group) (Mind, 2006). The research evidence however is problematic, since it is mostly based on service use statistics. The EMPIRIC study suggests a much lower incidence of severe mental illness than admission figures imply.

African-Caribbean people are, however, more likely to be held under the Mental Health Act and are more likely to receive medication rather than be offered therapies such as psychotherapy. They are also over-represented in special hospitals, secure institutions, medium secure units and prisons. Again, campaigning groups suggest that statutory services fail to engage effectively with African-Caribbean people. Mental health outcomes of black patients are shown to be poorer in terms of readmissions. Poorer clinical outcome has been associated with living alone, unemployment, conviction and imprisonment.

Evidence on the Asian community is inconsistent, with many suggesting that mental health problems are unrecognised. Suicide is low among Asian men and older people, but high in young Asian women compared with other ethnic groups.

The recent focus on mental health services has highlighted many significant areas of concern in relation to primary care. Many people with mental health problems contact their GP, or another member of the primary healthcare team. However, this does not appear to be true for all black and minority ethnic groups. According to the National Institute for Mental Health in England (Sashidharan, 2003):

- Research suggests that there are no major variations in registration with GPs and overall consultation rates between minority ethnic groups and the majority population. However, the capacity of GPs to recognise psychiatric disorders in Black and ethnic minority patients appears to be more limited than in others. There are indications that consultation rates for mental disorders, in particular, anxiety and depression, may be reduced in some minority groups, such as among South Asians and the Chinese. Most recent evidence shows that Irish people had particularly high rates of consulting GPs for psychological problems.
- Chinese groups tend to access their GP only after long delays and the GP is the first contact person for less than 40% of all individuals. Many individuals from minority ethnic groups encounter barriers when seeking help – including language, the discrepancy between the patient's and doctor's views as to the nature of the presenting symptoms, cultural barriers to assessment produced by the reliance on a narrow biomedical approach, lack of knowledge about statutory services, and lack of access to bilingual health professionals.
- Black and South Asian patients are less likely to have mental health problems recognised by their GP or the nature of their presentation wrongly attributed to mental illness. GPs acknowledge that they feel

less involved in the care of patients with severe mental illness from minority ethnic groups. There is also evidence that GPs' decisions to refer patients with mental health problems to specialist services are influenced by the patient's ethnicity.

- Police involvement and compulsory admissions for black and minority ethnic groups are strongly associated with the absence of GP involvement.

Western approaches to mental health treatment may be unsuitable and culturally inappropriate to meet the needs of some members of Asian communities.

Difficulties in interpreting evidence on mental health and ethnicity

Behaviour that might attract labels of mental illness could be a culturally acceptable way of accounting for misfortune or expressing distress. Since minority ethnic groups experience racism in everyday life, ranging from the fear and actuality of violent assault, to discrimination in education and the labour market, differences in rates of mental illness may not be 'cultural' at all, but an entirely explicable by-product of disproportionate exposure to societal stressors. Since minority ethnic groups are disproportionately located in lower income groups, and have higher rates of unemployment, their over-representation in some mental health categories could be an artefact of these other statistical associations. Mental health figures are frequently based on contact with treatment services, which in itself may tell us little about the real incidence in communities. Racist stereotypes, especially of the alleged 'dangerous' African-Caribbean male, may themselves account for phenomena such as the over-representation of males of African-Caribbean descent in mental health detention, in receiving electro-convulsive therapy and drug therapies, and their under-representation in access to talking therapies.

To the extent that wider society retains elements both of racism, and of discrimination against those with mental health problems, both minority ethnic status and having a mental illness are potentially mutually reinforcing sources of being stigmatised.

Examples of 'racialising' mental health issues include:

- Assumptions that certain ethnic groups automatically benefit from large extended kinship networks which will protect them against mental illnesses such as depression.
- Assumptions that difficulties such as conflict between generations or

conflicts within families are cultural rather than common to family and inter-generational relations of all ethnic groups.

- Attribution to 'culture' factors behind mental health that are to do with material and social factors (such as poverty, housing, unemployment, experience of racism)
- Attribution to 'culture', factors associated with mental health that derive from the interaction of health services and minority ethnic groups. For example, Nazroo (1997) found that African-Caribbean people who scored high on a depression scale were much less likely to be receiving treatment than were their White counterparts, even though they had consulted their GPs at the same rate.

Culture-bound syndromes or culture-bound medicine?

One particular controversy surrounding ethnicity and mental health is the notion that there may be mental health problems that are specific to certain cultures: the so-called 'culture-bound' syndromes. Thus one approach to ethnicity and the practice of psychiatric medicine is to list 'culture-bound' syndromes (such as 'soul loss' or 'semen loss') as specific to particular ethnic groups (see Dein, 1997). However, others have countered that conditions such as anorexia nervosa, bulimia, Type-A behaviour (chronically struggling against time, sense of failure in achieving goals, ambition, impatience in personal relationships) and even depression may equally be 'Western' culture-bound syndromes. Sumathipala et al (2004) suggest that on closer examination, these so-called culture-bound syndromes, whether Eastern or Western, are neither exotic nor rare and frequently occur across many different cultures. The issue seems to be of avoiding two equally problematic positions: universalistic conceptions and culturally essentialist conceptions of mental health.

- Universalism: in this view, there are true categories of mental health experience called, for example, such things as 'depression'. These occur in all cultures, but may take different forms or be expressed in different ways.
- Cultural essentialism: in this view, each person is situated within their own culture, with that culture determining the boundaries of their experience, producing its own unique distinctive type of illness.

However, it is possible that neither of these views is adequate for responding to that domain of interest we might call mental distress, as we can see from the case of Muslim and Sikh women of Punjabi descent discussed below.

Punjabi women and 'thinking too much with one's heart'

Common misconceptions are that women of South Asian descent:

- Are protected against poor mental health by strong families.
- Do not experience depression.
- If they do experience depression, they do not recognise it.
- They fail to present it to doctors.
- They disguise it by presenting with physical symptoms.
- They do not understand the relationship between mental states and physical symptoms.

However, according to Fenton and Sadiq-Sangster (1996) none of these ideas was born out by the evidence of their sample of (Muslim and Sikh) Punjabi women.

Instead the women spoke about a core experience of mental distress: 'thinking too much with one's heart' (so 'stop thinking so much' advice was unhelpful and inappropriate). On the one hand the women reported a number of symptoms (loss of purpose; loss of appetite; loss of sense of self-worth; overwhelming tiredness; bodily aches and pains; suicidal thoughts; sleeplessness; not coping with daily tasks) that might be regarded as core symptoms of a medical model of 'depression'. On the other hand, although they recognised the medical term mental illness, it was not a good fit for what they described, not least because thinking too much with one's heart could affect the mind or lead to mental illness (so it was not merely their term for mental illness, it was a qualitatively different concept). Thus although 'thinking too much with one's heart' was a core experience of distress, it did not map on to a medical model of depression.

If we look further at one of the detailed comments of the Punjabi women, we can begin to trace how a number of challenges in the practice of medicine manifest themselves.

The health visitor tells me to go out, but I don't feel like it – I have to face this sort of trouble (referring to the 'Paki' calls and stone-throwing). I am so upset, my mind (mera dimaag) is going bad ... I was in such a state ... I was shaking all over ... I went to the doctor and told him all my problems. He said really your problem is the house problem and that you worry too much (about your children). But (the doctor is English) ... you see I can explain myself in English somewhat but I can't tell him how

I am feeling – what is in my heart – as I am doing to you now... all the small things in our language. I can't say how I am feeling in my heart ... I can't get the right words.

(Fenton and Sadiq-Sangster, 1996: 76)

Thus the mother is subject to poor quality housing, ill-suited for her needs but her income is too low to change this situation herself. Moreover, she is subject to racist abuse and her way of describing her distress at the racism and socio-economic position she is in is 'thinking too much with her heart'.

More generally, since Pubjabi women's problems lie in social relations, they may present physical problems to the doctor (because that is conceived of as within the doctor's realm) but not present mental health problems (firstly because 'thinking with one's heart' is referred to as a potential cause of mental health problems although it is not one and the same thing as mental health problems, and secondly because this is not an illness for which there is a doctor's cure). This can then be mistaken for either patients not recognising their depression at all or misunderstanding it as 'somatisation', that is, representing mental health problems as physical ones, and stereotypes about South Asian women and depression are confirmed in the doctor's mind. The women cannot express their views to the doctor because there are no professional interpretation services available (a problem of service provision not of mental health). The particular Punjabi woman is unhelpfully told not to think (worry) too much (which misses the relevant domain of experience because thinking in the head is not the same experience as thinking with one's heart).

To summarise this complex chain of events:

- Neither a universalist model of depression, nor a cultural essentialist model of 'culture-bound syndromes' adequately captures the complexity of a core experience of distress: 'thinking too much with one's heart'.
- Inadequate interpretation and lack of bilingual health services means the complexity of the needs cannot be communicated to the doctor.
- For the Punjabi women, the solution to their social distress is not seen to lie with prescription drugs: 'There is no tablet for my sorrow', 'Should I keep taking the tablets or go to Pakistan?'
- The mental health of Punjabi women in the UK is racialised. That is, the effects of stressors of racism, housing and poverty become obscured such that specific social conditions become viewed as naturally occurring characteristics of 'Asian culture'.
- The women talk about their families, their hopes, prayers, and sorrow,

but in a fashion about which it is extremely difficult to be precise. They do not talk about themselves. Thus the sense of self and self-worth that is an important way of characterising depression in the UK may itself have ethnocentric elements.

GOOD PRACTICE: Mental health

Antenna Outreach (Barnet, Enfield and Haringey Mental Health NHS Trust): Antenna provides a culturally sensitive outreach service to people of African and Caribbean origin who are aged 16–25 years. It offers support to families and carers, and awareness raising within Tottenham and Edmonton to a range of service providers. The project visits schools, churches and mosques, youth services and educational centres in the borough to raise awareness about mental health issues with people from ethnic minorities, to tackle stigma and to cultivate a more accessible, sensitive approach to mental health issues. It contributes to a school health-mentoring programme. A community event attracting up to 500 people is held annually to raise awareness about mental health issues within the local community. The youth group also visits youth clubs, sixth form colleges and community centres to promote its work.

Substance use

In this section we look at the issue of minority ethnic groups and alcohol, tobacco and other substance use. We begin with the issue of alcohol use. Unless otherwise stated, the evidence referred to in the section on alcohol is derived from a synthesis of numerous of national and local studies on Black and minority ethnic groups and alcohol produced by Alcohol Concern (2003).

Alcohol

The most widely abused substance in the UK is alcohol. One factor worthy of comment here is that even literature that seeks to understand the experiences of Black and minority ethnic groups with respect to the use of alcohol refers to the 'general population' as a reference point against which rates of usage among minority groups are judged. But what this means is that people of White ethnicities (mainly, but not exclusively, of English, Scottish, and Welsh descent) are not labelled as having a 'cultural' problem with alcohol simply because they are themselves the reference group who are taken as a 'norm'. If this were any other issue, or any other ethnic group, most commentators would be saying that White 'cultures' are deficient because they are associated with high levels of alcohol consumption among both men and women, and that these high levels are associated with violence, crime, family break-up, accidents, and workplace absenteeism, and that, as such, place unwarranted demands onto health services.

The implication of *Figure 7.1* is that 30% of men in the general population exceed the weekly safe drinking levels of 21 units, compared with only around half that proportion for African-Caribbean and Indian men. Very few men of Chinese, Pakistani or Bangladeshi descent reported unsafe drinking levels. The one exception to conflating White ethnicity with the reference group is to identify 34% of men of Irish descent as exceeding safe drinking levels. Likewise 16% women in the 'general population' report exceeding the level of 14 units per week of alcohol, compared to Black Caribbean (9%), Chinese (4%) and minimal numbers of women of Indian, Pakistani or Bangladeshi descent.

However, despite the apparent overall higher levels of prevalence, a number of local studies, collated by Alcohol Concern (2003), suggest that patterns of drinking may be changing in younger South Asian communities;

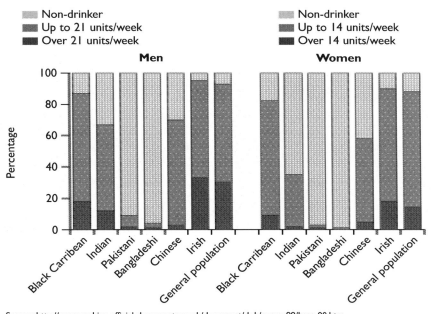

Source: http://www.archive.official-documents.co.uk/document/doh/survey99/hses-00.htm
The Health of Minority Ethnic Groups 1999 (Health Survey for England). Crown copyright material.

Figure 7.1. Weekly reported consumption of alcohol by ethnic group, 1999.

that overall figures for an ethnic group hide variation within that group (one study identified high levels of drinking among Sikh men); that among the smaller proportions of certain ethnic groups the minority who do drink are consuming especially high levels of alcohol (a local study found 10% of Muslim men in one Midlands city reported drinking, with high levels of consumption among those who did drink).

Substance misuse is correlated with a number of other social factors such as unemployment, homelessness, family break-up, and crime. Because correlation (association) is not causation, it is not clear to what extent the substance misuse is the antecedent of the social misfortune, or whether the substance use is an (ultimately) counter-productive coping response to a social ill. However, those from minority ethnic groups may have some different routes into substance abuse. For instance, an African-Caribbean woman relates the origins of her drinking problem to experiences of racism and the self-loathing this engendered in her.

When I was 10 I went into a children's home outside London which had a fairly large percentage of Black children and yet all the staff were White. I remember one house mother saying to me, 'You know, you're all right, if you could get rid of your accent.' [...] I remember this house warden saying, 'You're not like the rest of them,' meaning Black people. Until I was about 17 or 18 I was really screwed up because I didn't like being Black. I remember when I was about 9, I'd wish they'd invent a new kind of medicine that would turn me White.

Wolfson and Murray (1986: 24)

Furthermore, two main resources in resisting racism are the family and the sense of community moral superiority, of being better people than the ethnic groups perpetrating the racism (see Culley et al, 2001). In respect of the latter resource, it is interesting to note that losing identity with one's religion was an indicator associated with drinking for both men and women in ethnic minority groups. Problem drinking cuts across both of these important resources. Since about 40% of the ethnic minority women accessing drugs and alcohol services may be doing so because of their partner's drinking, rather than their own, the issues of gender and domestic violence also become pertinent.

One factor that has undermined provision of services to minority ethnic users is the lack of Black and minority ethnic workers within drugs and alcohol services, and a lack of interpretation and translation services, although both are beginning to change. Specialist drugs and alcohol services may offer a 'menu' of treatment options from detoxification, abstinence goal models, talking therapies, counselling and harm-reduction strategies.

Table 7.1. Assessment of drinkers by report of risky substance-related activities

Risks to self	Risks to others	Other risks
Gone with strangers	Caused an accident	Been thrown out of somewhere
Walked alone	Aggressiveness	Police stop
Gambled	Been in a fight	Been convicted
Unsafe sex	Damaged things	Lost days work
Taken other drugs	Neglected a child	Worked poorly
Argued with gatekeeper figures	Spent family money	Been warned at work
Had an accident	Driven while drunk	Family criticism
Passed out		Feelings of shame

Source: Alcohol Concern (2003)

Increasingly, in pursuit of a model of intervention that keeps clients within their local community (to which they would eventually have to return even if referred to specialist services), rather than intervening directly, specialist workers support generalists such as family doctors on the basis that they have the skills, the local knowledge and the credibility to work with those experiencing problems and to keep them in their community. *Table 7.1*, originally developed as a research tool, may be of some use in assessing a patient with problem substance use such as alcohol.

Tobacco

Cigarette smoking is another issue where it would be easy to fall into the trap of racialisation. The ethnic groups reported as having higher rates of smoking among men (Bangladeshi 44%, Irish 39%, and Black Caribbean 35%) all experience high levels of material deprivation, unemployment, and occupation in low skilled monotonous jobs with little control over the flow and pace of the work – all factors equally associated with high rates of smoking. Twenty seven per cent of men in the general population smoke cigarettes, slightly fewer Pakistani and Indian men smoke (26% and 23%, respectively), with lowest males rates among the Chinese (17%). For women the Irish group (33%) were more likely to smoke cigarettes than women in the general population (27%), or Black Caribbean women (25%). Women in all other ethnic groups had low rates of smoking at

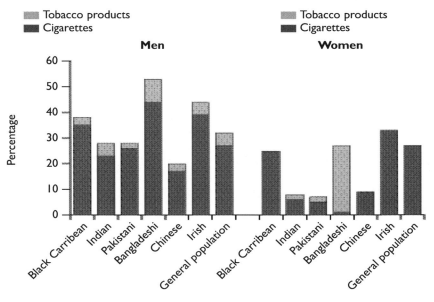

Source: http://www.archive.official-documents.co.uk/document/doh/survey99/hses-00.htm
The Health of Minority Ethnic Groups 1999 (Health Survey for England) Crown copyright material.

Figure 7.2: Reported rates of tobacco use by ethnic group, 1999.

below or well below 10%.

Including chewing tobacco products increased rates of overall tobacco use (i.e. smoking and chewing combined) for some South Asian groups, especially for Bangladeshi men (19%) and Bangladeshi women (26%).

Chewing drugs

Although health professionals will be very familiar with the effects of cigarette smoking, other forms of drugs that are chewed may be less familiar.

Betel nut and paan

Betel nut comes from the betel palm. Sliced or ground, it is chewed for 20 minutes. The high level of alkaloids it contains is responsible for the nicotine-like effects. It may be mixed with lime (calcium oxide) to maximise extraction of the active ingredient.

On the Indian Sub-Continent betel nut is mixed with tobacco and/ or spices for flavour and is known as 'paan'. Regular chewing leads to gums, teeth and stools being stained red. It has been linked to oral cancer (independently of its mixture with chewing tobacco) and to mouth ulcers and gum disease. According to MedlinePlus there are a number of possible interactions of betel nut with other substances.

- The effects of anticholinergic drugs may decrease when used in combination with betel nut or its constituent arecoline. Use with cholinergic drugs may cause toxicity (salivation, incontinence, sweating, diarrhoea, vomiting, or fever). Betel nut may slow or raise the heart rate, and could alter the effects of drugs that slow the heart, such as beta-blockers, calcium channel blockers, or digoxin.
- Based on animal studies, betel nut may alter blood sugar levels. Caution is advised when using medications that may also alter blood sugar. Patients taking drugs for diabetes by mouth or using insulin should be monitored closely by a qualified healthcare provider. Medication adjustments may be necessary.
- Based on laboratory and animal research, betel nut may increase the effects of monoamine oxidase inhibitors, angiotensin-converting enzyme inhibitors, phenothiazines, cholesterol-lowering drugs, or stimulant drugs. Betel may increase or decrease the effects of anti-glaucoma eye drops. Reliable human study is lacking in these areas.

Khat (chat or jat)

The chewing of khat is especially associated with the Somali refugee community. The leaves of the plant are chewed over several hours, producing mild stimulant and mild euphoric effects. The active ingredient breaks down over 72 hours, producing a premium on the freshness of the leaves. It is particularly popular among men of Somali descent, and may be chewed in social gatherings in khat houses, a closed space for chewing, sharing coffee and cigarettes, and talking.

Problems may have less to do with the active ingredients, than the money khat use takes from already low income households, and the socially isolating effects of khat houses that reinforce the social exclusion of an already socially excluded group.

Since khat use is a highly social activity abstinence is an unlikely goal, and harm-reduction advice has been produced that focuses on reducing the frequency of sessions, not sharing cups or cigarettes, not retaining a wad of khat in the mouth for long periods and maintaining mouth hygiene.

The following quotation suggests the manner by which khat use becomes a social activity; it combines a shared longing for the homeland by using a product imported from the homeland and with escape from the everyday challenges of poverty and racism. The sharing of khat, coffee, cigarettes and drinks involves a physical coming together in an enclosed space.

A small flat, 20 to 30 men all chewing (khat) and smoking .... little ventilation, bottles of coke lying around ... tea and coffee ... and this scene continues every night for 10 to 12 hours at a time .... As we get stimulated we all talk at once ... we are again in Somalia ... we share stories of home ... we remember ... and imagine scenes from home before the war ... we dream of returning ... and for a while escape the reality that is our life now ...

Saloo (2001:67)

GOOD PRACTICE: Harm reduction and khat use

Ealing Drug Education Project: The project works with the African, Caribbean, Somali and South Asian communities in Southall and other parts of Ealing to ensure that the range of cultural and language needs are met appropriately and that relevant drug education resources are used. It provides educational sessions in Gurmukhi Punjabi, Mirpuri Punjabi, Urdu, Bengali, Gujarati, Somali, English and Farsi. It works both through officers and trained community volunteers. In particular it has produced a booklet in English and Somali focusing on harm reduction in chewing khat.

Drug and Alcohol Action Programme Ltd, KAS House, Unit K, Middlesex Business Centre, Bridge Road, Southall, Middlesex UB2 4AB Telephone: 0208 843 0945

Cannabis

Perhaps the most contentious of all the links between substance use and mental health problems is the controversial diagnosis of 'cannabis psychosis', and whether use of cannabis is a cause of later onset of schizophrenia or depression. In particular, controversy has surrounded claims that high rates of psychosis are linked to higher cannabis consumption among those of African-Caribbean descent. Challenges to such a link are that no significant differences in level of cannabis use have been found between Black and White patients with psychosis, and that, contrary to popular stereotypes, levels of cannabis use may be lower among African-Caribbeans than Whites, even though levels of reported schizophrenia are higher (Sharpley et al, 2001).

It is difficult to reconcile these opposing sets of arguments, but what little consensus there is appears to amount to:

- Cannabis use before 18 may increase risks of later mental health problems.

- Cannabis use by those predisposed to mental health problems may increase risks.
- Cannabis use for those who already have mental health problems may exacerbate them.

According to UK Cannabis Internet Activists (2006) there are methodological problems with the interpretation of evidence on cannabis use.

- There is a confusion of correlation and causation. Any association of cannabis use and schizophrenia could be that cannabis causes schizophrenia or that schizophrenia causes people to misuse drugs such as cannabis, or it may be that family break-up or unemployment may independently drive both, leading to an apparent relationship.
- The publication of research studies increased around the period leading up to the political struggle over the legal reclassification of cannabis.
- Most studies rely on self-report of use of an illegal drug.
- One active chemical in cannabis is tetrahydrocannabinol (THC). However, cannabis also contains cannabidiol (CBD). CBD seems to have good anti-psychotic properties and calls into question any studies based on THC alone.
- The context of some cannabis use – a counter-cultural lifestyle – may lead to exclusions (from school, employment, family) and inclusions (into a world of illegal activities and into the criminal justice system) that themselves are correlated with increased rates of schizophrenia. In this argument the causal agent is the illegal status of the drug, not the chemicals of the drug itself.
- Poorly controlled studies in which correlations between cannabis use and schizophrenia turned out to be because a proportion of those who had used cannabis had also used amphetamines, a less disputed antecedent to psychosis.
- There is selective presentation or amplification of only one part of complex and contradictory evidence: Patton et al (2002) found early use of cannabis among teenage girls associated with increased depression and anxiety, but a trend to decreased prevalence of depression among teenage boys reporting cannabis use. Arsenault et al (2002) found statistical association of cannabis use by age 15 with schizophrenia but no statistically significant increase for those who delayed starting until 18. Zammit et al (2002) found an association between army conscripts aged 18–20 who had used cannabis more than 50 times and later schizophrenia, but a trend to decreased rates of schizophrenia among those who reported using between 11 and 50 times.

- Long-term epidemiological studies show a marked decrease in rates of schizophrenia coinciding with widespread increases in recreational use of cannabis in the UK.
- Using their data Degenhardt et al (2003) concluded that 'cannabis use does not appear to be causally related to the incidence of schizophrenia'. However they did find that it is possible that 'its use may precipitate disorders in persons who are vulnerable to developing psychosis and worsen the course of the disorder among those who have already developed it'.

Key points

- Neither biological (genetic) nor 'cultural' differences between ethnic groups, nor experience of migration are convincing explanations for patterns of mental health among the UK's minority ethnic groups.
- Mental health problems in all ethnic groups are associated with a range of adverse socio-economic factors associated with disadvantage and discrimination and these can also be a cause of social exclusion.
- There are significant barriers to minority ethnic groups seeking and successfully accessing mental health services. Furthermore, there are significant ethnic differences in the experience of services and in the outcome of service interventions.
- Alcohol use is most problematic among the various White cultures in the UK, with minority ethnic use being considerably lower.

References

Alcohol Concern (2003) Alcohol drinking among black and minority ethnic communities (BME) in the United Kingdom. *Acquire* (Alcohol Concern's Quarterly Information and Research Bulletin) **Spring**

Arseneault L, Cannon M, Poulton R, Murray R, Caspi A, Moffitt TE (2002) Cannabis use in adolescence and risk for adult psychosis: Longitudinal prospective study. *British Medical Journal* **325**(7374): 1212–3

Culley LA, Dyson SM, han-Ying S, Young W (2001) Caribbean nurses and racism in the NHS. In Culley L, Dyson,SM (eds) *Ethnicity and Nursing Practice*. Palgrave, Basingstoke

Degenhardt L, Hall W, Lynskey M (2003) Testing hypotheses about the relationship between cannabis use and psychosis. *Drug and Alcohol Dependence* **71**(1):37–48

Dein S (1997) ABC of mental health: Mental health in a multi-ethnic society. *British Medical Journal* **315**: 473–6

Fenton S, Sadiq-Sangster A (1996) Culture, relativism and the expression of mental distress: South Asian women in Britain. *Sociology of Health and Illness* **18**(1): 66–85

MedlinePlus http://www.nlm.nih.gov/medlineplus/druginfo/natural/patient-betelnut.html [accessed 23rd June 2006]

Mind (2006) *The mental health of the African Caribbean community in Britain.* Available from: http://www.mind.org.uk/help/people_groups_and_communities/ mental_health_of_the_african_caribbean_community_in_britain [Last accessed 18 August 2009]

National Institute for Mental Health in England (2003) *Inside Outside – Improving Mental HEalth Services for Black and Minority Ethnic Communities in England. The Case for Action.* www.nimhe.org.uk

Nazroo JY (1997) *Ethnicity and Mental Health: Findings from a National Community Survey.* Policy Studies Institute, London

Patton GC, Coffey C, Carlin JB, Degenhardt L, Lynskey M, Hall W (2002) Cannabis use and mental health in young people: Cohort study. *British Medical Journal* **325**(7374):1183–4

Saloo F (2001) *Khat Use Amongst Somali Refugees Living in Leicester.* Unpublished Thesis, MA Applied Health Studies, De Montfort University, Leicester

Sashidharan S (2003) *Inside Outside: Improving mental health services for black and minority ethnic communities in England.* Department of Health, London.

Sharpley MS, Hutchinson G, Murray RM, McKenzie K (2001) Bringing in the social environment: Understanding the excess of psychosis among the African-Caribbean population in England. *British Journal of Psychiatry* **178**: s60–8

Sproston K, Nazroo JDS (2000) *Ethnic Minority Psychiatric Illness Rates in the Community (EMPIRIC) - Quantitative Report.* The Stationery Office, London

Sumathipala A, Siribaddana SH, Bhugra D (2004) Culture-bound syndromes: The story of dhat syndrome. *British Journal of Psychiatry* **184**: 200–9

UK Cannabis Internet Activists (2006) *Cannabis and Mental Health.* Available from: http://www.ikcia.org.culture/effects/psychosisandschizophrenia.php [Last accessed 27 June 2006]

Wolfson D, Murray J (1986) *Women and Dependency: Women's Personal Accounts of Drug and Alcohol Problems.* DAWN (Drugs Alcohol Women Nationally), London

Zammit S, Allebeck P, Andreasson S, Lundberg I, Lewis G (2002) Self-reported cannabis use as a risk factor for schizophrenia in Swedish conscripts of 1969: Historical cohort study. *British Medical Journal* **325**(7374): 1199–2003

Further reading

Bhui K (2003) Ethnic variations in pathways to specialist mental health services in the United Kingdom: A systematic review. *British Journal of Psychiatry* **182**: 105–16

Department of Health (2005) *Delivering Race Equality in Mental Health Care.* Department of Health, London

Keating F (2007) *African and Caribbean Men and Mental Health.* Race Equality Foundation, London

National Institute for Mental Health in England (2003) *Inside Outside – Improving Mental Health Services for Black and Minority Ethnic Communities in England. The Case for Action.* Department of Health, London

Savva S, Edwards G (2003) Ethnicity and Substance Abuse: Prevention and Intervention. *Addiction* **98**(6). 859–9. doi:10.1046/j.1360-0443.2003.04404.x

CHAPTER 8

Refugees and asylum seekers

In this chapter, we examine the challenges facing two particular groups within minority ethnic communities, namely refugees and asylum seekers. The circumstances of their migration, and the uncertainties of their legal status within the UK, means that these groups are faced with additional challenges in accessing good healthcare and in achieving good health status.

Definitions

Asylum seekers are people who have fled persecution in their homeland, have arrived in another country, made themselves known to the authorities, and exercised the legal right to apply for asylum.

Refugees are people whose asylum applications have been successful and who are allowed to stay in another country having proved that they would face persecution if they returned home.

Failed asylum seekers are people whose asylum applications have been turned down and are awaiting return to their country.

Illegal immigrants are people who have arrived in another country, intentionally not made themselves known to the authorities and have no legal basis for remaining.

Economic migrants are people who move to another country to work.

Asylum and immigration

Home Office figures show that most settlements in the UK are for family reasons, typically when someone marries a foreign national. The next largest category of settlement is work-related. People who have been legally resident and working in the UK for five years can ask for permanent residential status. Only around 15% of settlements are people who have been accepted as refugees.

The UK context

- The UK is home to 3% of the world's refugees (289 100 out of 9.2 million). Two thirds of refugees are living in developing countries;

- Africa and Asia alone host over 70% of the world's refugees. The UK is ranked 14th in the league table of EU countries for the number of asylum applications per head of population.
- The UK asylum system is strictly controlled and complex. It is very difficult to get asylum. Under the new asylum model, most asylum interviews will take place five days after an application is lodged, giving applicants just a few days to prepare their case in full.
- Most asylum seekers in Britain are single men, under the age of 40, although worldwide most refugees are women. Many families in Britain are without one parent, who may be missing or dead, and there are appreciable numbers of unaccompanied minors. Numbers from each country fluctuate principally according to the local human rights situation.
- While asylum seekers want to work and support themselves, they are not allowed to work for the first 12 months of their application.
- Asylum seekers are much more likely to be the victims of crime than the perpetrators. A study conducted by Refugee Action (www.refugee-action.org.uk) found that one in five of their clients had experienced some kind of harassment, while 83% of asylum-seeking women do not go out at night for fear of being abused and harassed.
- Applications for asylum, excluding dependants, fell by 24% in 2005 to 25 710 (see *Figure 8.1*). The nationalities accounting for the highest numbers of applicants were Iranian, Somali, Eritrean, Chinese and Afghan.

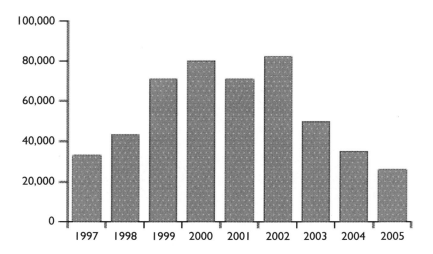

Figure 8.1. Applications received for asylum, UK 1997–2005 (excluding dependents). From: Home Office (2006).

- In 2007 applications for asylum fell by a further 1% to 23 430. The nationalities accounting for the highest numbers of applicants were Afghan, Iranian, Chinese, Iraqi and Eritrean
- Most asylum applications are refused. In 2005 83% were refused; 7% were granted asylum and 12% were granted humanitarian protection or discretionary leave (see *Figure 8.2*). In 2006 10% were granted asylum and in 2007 this rose to 16%. The proportion granted Humanitarian Protection (HP) or Discretionary Leave (DL) decreased to 10% in 2007.
- At the end of 2007, the top three asylum seeker dispersal towns in England were Birmingham (1960), Leeds (1760) and Manchester (1310). Asylum seekers were also dispersed to Scotland (Glasgow City, 3905) and Wales (2205).

(Home Office, 2008)

The most up to date analyses of statistics on asylum seekers and refugees are available from the Information Centre About Asylum Seekers and Refugees (UCAR), an independent research body based at City University London (www.icar.org.uk).

Humanitarium protection and discretionary leave

Humanitarian protection is leave granted to a person who would, if removed, face, in the country of return, a serious risk to life arising from the death penalty; unlawful killing; or torture or inhuman or degrading treatment or punishment. If a person has been refused asylum he or she may still be

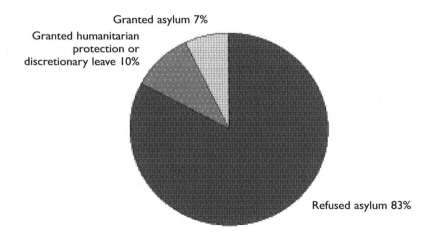

Granted asylum 7%

Granted humanitarian protection or discretionary leave 10%

Refused asylum 83%

Figure 8.2. Initial UK asylum outcome decisions 2005. From: Home Office (2006).

considered for this status. Humanitarian protection is normally granted for a period of three years, after which the person can apply for indefinite leave to remain. A person who is granted humanitarian protection is allowed to work and has access to public funds.

Discretionary leave can be considered for people who have not been considered for international protection, or have been excluded. Discretionary leave may be granted if, for example, the applicant is an unaccompanied asylum seeking child (UASC) for whom adequate reception arrangements in the child's own country are not available, or if the child is able to demonstrate particularly compelling reasons why removal would not be appropriate. Discretionary leave can be granted for a period of three years or less; for UASCs it can be granted for three years or up until their 18th birthday, whichever comes first.

These categories have now replaced the status, exceptional leave to remain.

Diversity

It is important to recognise that asylum seekers and refugees are not a homogenous group of people. They come from different countries and will have a wide range of experiences that may affect their health and nutritional status. Many asylum seekers are highly skilled and had a previously high standard of living. However, the circumstances of life in the UK undermine both physical and mental health. Since they are not allowed to work, they are forced to rely on State support, which is set at 70% of income support. Thus, many asylum seekers are living in poverty (Refugee Action, 2006) and most are housed in poor quality 'hard to let' accommodation in deprived areas. Popular reporting and commentary about asylum seekers and refugees is often hostile, unbalanced and factually incorrect, leading to community mistrust and conflict.

Media reporting is characterised by the use of inaccurate and provocative terminology, including the use of derogatory labels to describe asylum seekers. The tabloid press particularly fails to distinguish between economic migrants and asylum seekers and refugees (Buchanan et al, 2003).

Healthcare needs

Restrictions on access and entitlements to health and social care can have a devastating impact on already vulnerable refugees who have come to the UK for protection. The health of asylum seekers may actually get worse after entry to the UK. The British Medical Association (2002) however, argues that a significant number of asylum seekers are prone to particular health problems, such as a range of communicable diseases (tuberculosis, hepatitis, HIV/AIDS), the physical effects of war and torture (rape/sexual assault, landmine injuries, beatings and malnutrition) and social and psychological problems (depression, stress and anxiety, racial harassment). It concludes that from the point of entry to the UK, not enough is being done to safeguard the health of asylum seekers. Basic medical testing does not routinely take place, which means that tuberculosis often goes undiagnosed, those suffering from psychological effects of torture are not always referred to specialist centres; and unaccompanied children are not given appropriate vaccinations and immunisations.

Studies suggest that one in six refugees has a physical health problem severe enough to affect his or her life and two thirds have experienced anxiety or depression. Refugees from countries without a developed primary care system may be unused to hospital referrals and this can create tensions with healthcare workers. 'Disentangling the web of history, symptoms – which may be minimised or exaggerated for a range of reasons – and current coping mechanisms requires patience and often several sessions' (Burnett and Peel, 2001). Hepatitis A and B and meningitis may be more prevalent dependent on country of origin, while HIV prevalence is likely to mirror that in the home country. However, in some cases women have higher rates of infection where they have been used as sex slaves or subject to gang rape. Asylum seekers may be scared to disclose their HIV status as they may feel it will influence their asylum claim. Gastrointestinal symptoms are common and there is also a risk of substance misuse as a coping strategy. Children and adults may be incompletely immunised and dental problems are common (Aspinall, 2006).

Data on the prevalence of chronic conditions is poor, although high rates of diabetes, hypertension and coronary heart disease are reported in refugees from eastern Europe. Estimates of the prevalence of disability vary from 3% to 10%. Significant numbers of asylum seekers have experienced torture (estimates vary from 5% to 30%) and local studies report that injuries caused by persecution are one of the most frequent concerns among asylum seekers (Apsinall, 2006).

Psychological symptoms

Many asylum seekers will have been forced to leave behind key family members and have little knowledge of their fate. Many have been subjected to oppressive conditions and torture. People may show symptoms of depression and anxiety, panic attacks and agoraphobia, exacerbated by social isolation and poverty. It is important to be aware that the expression of mental distress and its treatment is culture bound and health professionals may need to seek specialist help in understanding different cultural frameworks for seeking help (see Chapter 7). Counselling, for example, is an unfamiliar concept for many asylum seekers and may be rejected or ineffective if it is not culturally sensitive. A list of specialist mental health services for asylum seekers is available from the Information Centre about Asylum and Refugees in the UK (http://www.icar.webbler. co.uk/). Other information is available from the Help for Asylum Seekers and Refugees Portal (http://www.mentalhealth.harpweb.org/). This latter site has been designed to help health professionals to assist asylum seekers with mental health issues. It includes information on:

- Crisis intervention.
- Rights and awareness.
- Dos and don'ts in treating asylum seekers and refugees.
- Pathways to support (practical tools and guidelines).
- A guide to mental health problems.
- Cultural understandings (information on the role of culture in the context of mental health and well-being).

Women

Displaced women are particularly vulnerable to assault, sexual harassment and rape. Tensions of life in refugee communities may make marital breakdown and domestic violence more common and women may be coping with sole responsibility for children. Women are less likely to be English speakers and may easily become isolated and lonely. Uptake of screening and other health promotion programmes may be limited, and women need to be offered sexual health care, family planning and maternity care that is sensitive to their needs (Burnett and Peel, 2001). A recent report for the Maternity Alliance (McLeish 2002) found that asylum seekers and their babies survived in a support system that fell far short of meeting their most basic needs for adequate food and safe shelter. Already lonely, disorientated and grieving, half of the women also experienced neglect, disrespect and racism from the maternity services.

Children

Many children seeking asylum who arrive in the UK will have already experienced considerable physical and mental hardship. Not only will they have lost their homes, schools and friends, some children will have witnessed horrific events, and many of them have spent months in hiding. Some children will have been tortured. If children are with a relative other than a parent, their application for refugee status may be refused. Children may also arrive in the UK without any accompanying adults. Many asylum seekers are detained when they arrive in the UK and this can cause extreme psychological distress for detained children who rarely have access to appropriate education.

Some children may have to take on the role of head of the household because of the acquisition of language skills, or because their parents are unable to fulfil this role because of their own distress.

Refugee children often attain good levels of childhood immunisation, although it can be difficult for GPs to construct an accurate record of immunisations. Children may have been given cholera or measles vaccination in refugee camps or come with records that are indecipherable and parents may not be familiar with the concept or range of diseases for which vaccination is available.

Refugee children are often traumatised by war. For example, Somali boys have often had the responsibility for the care and protection of others, carried weapons and witnessed atrocities. These experiences tend to accelerate their development whilst leaving them particularly vulnerable. They often do not see themselves as children but as young men and see school as beneath them. Many of these children are living with fragmented, reconstituted or new families in this country.

(Refugee Health Consortium, 1998)

GOOD PRACTICE: Women and children

Women: The POPPY Project was set up in 2003 to provide accommodation and support to women who have been trafficked into prostitution. It has 35 bed spaces in houses throughout London. POPPY also includes an outreach service to improve the safety and well-being of women from all over the UK who have been trafficked and who are in need of short-term support and advocacy. http://www.eaves4women.co.uk/POPPY_Project/POPPY_Project.php

Women and children: A number of excellent specialist resources for those working with women and children are available at: http://www.harpweb.org.uk/index.php. This site offers a range of resources for working with asylum seekers and refugees. It has specific content relating to the health and social care needs of men, women and children, and also includes some basic information about different cultures to assist in the development of culturally sensitive clinical practice. It contains practical tools including a model of hand-held records, a model welcome pack and instructions on taking medicines in several languages.

Communication

Having a trained advocate or interpreter is important, and use of family members, especially children, should be avoided if at all possible. (See *Chapter 4*). Telephone interpreters may be particularly important here because of the wide range of languages, and also because there may be a lack of trust in interpreters who may be seen to be allied to particular political groups.

Meeting healthcare needs

Most studies of asylum seekers and refugees identify barriers in accessing services, including primary care. In its report *Asylum seekers: Meeting their healthcare needs* the British Medical Association (2002) lists the following recommendations:

- The dispersal policy should be effectively managed so that asylum seekers receive adequate accommodation and are not moved from place to place. In this way, asylum seekers will be more likely to integrate into the community and access the services they require.
- Funding for asylum seekers should not be provided within existing general practitioner budgets as this will have a knock on effect on healthcare provision to the resident population. New money should be made available.
- Children should be educated within the local community as this improves integration with the host community and is therefore beneficial to their general wellbeing.
- More research is needed in order to progress the debate on the impact of UK immigration controls on health – this should include basic demographic characteristics of asylum seekers, health on entry to the UK, the impact on general practitioner practices and the cost-effectiveness of the Government's new proposals.
- The physical and mental health of all asylum seekers (including unaccompanied children) should be assessed and appropriate treatment and/or support given. Medical assessment should include testing for tuberculosis, Hepatitis A, B, C and HIV (with appropriate counselling), immunisation and vaccination assessment and referral to a specialist centre if there is any evidence of physical or psychological torture or maltreatment. The British Medical Association remains opposed to mandatory HIV testing for migrants. It believes that testing should be offered as part of a healthcare package, but informed consent will always be necessary.

GOOD PRACTICE: Access to healthcare

The Enfield Primary Care Trust and the London Borough of Enfield have jointly produced a booklet for refugees and asylum seekers. It helps the user understand how the healthcare system works in the UK and explains what healthcare everyone is entitled to and how to get it. It outlines what the first steps should be for a refugee or asylum seeker, from obtaining an HC1/2 to registering with a dentist.

ASSIST: This nurse-led service which provides healthcare to Leicester's asylum seekers began taking its first patients in June 2004. ASSIST is one of only a few services in the UK dedicated to primary care for asylum seekers. Key features of the service include providing interpreters and translation; specialist care for mental health and trauma; early intervention for mental health problems and specialist vaccination clinics.

- Trained interpreters or advocates, rather than family members or friends, should be used wherever possible if language is not shared.
- Asylum seekers should not normally be held in detention. This applies especially to families, children and pregnant women. Detention can remind torture victims of their experiences and compound the psychological damage/torment that they have already suffered.

Refugee community organisations

Community organisations can play an important role in the promotion and provision of health services to asylum seeker and refugees, although many remain under-resourced. Links to local resources are available from the Help for Asylum Seekers and Refugees Portal (http://www.harpweb.org.uk/index.php).

General information and resources

- HARPWEB (http://www.harpweb.org.uk/) consists of three websites, each developed in collaboration with health professionals working with asylum seekers and refugees in the UK. They are designed to enable easy access to the wealth of information, practical tools, and articles that have been written by healthcare professionals, non-governmental organisations, academics and research bodies with expert knowledge of working with asylum seekers and refugees, both in the UK and other countries.

- The Refugee Council provides up-to-date information on current issues around asylum seekers and refugees, the legal process of seeking asylum and rights to access NHS care (http://www.refugeecouncil.org.uk/).
- ICAR (Information Centre about Asylum and Refugees) provides detailed information about asylum statistics in the UK, population guides to the main refugee groups in the UK, lists of resources by region, and real life accounts of persecution and exile (http://www.icar.webbler.co.uk/).
- Home Office. Latest statistics are also available from the Home Office website (http://www.homeoffcie.gov.uk).
- Two useful handbooks for GPs are Burnett and Fassil (2002) and Fine and Cheal (2004).

The Department of Health's Asylum Seeker Co-ordination Team (ASCT)

The Department of Health's Asylum Seeker Co-ordination Team (ASCT) co-ordinates healthcare policy for asylum seekers and refugees. The team works across the Department of Health and other Government departments and with health workers and service planners in the field. The Depatment of Health website includes a series of resources (www.dh.gov.uk).

- *Caring for dispersed asylum seekers: A resource pack*. This document is aimed at helping local health and social care agencies to meet the needs of asylum seekers who are dispersed to their areas. Key concepts and entitlements are set out along with examples of good practice. Initiatives such as local development schemes, personal medical service pilots and the development of health assessments for asylum seekers at induction centres are included.
- *Table of entitlement to NHS treatment*. This table includes the most up-to-date information on rights to access health services.
- *Patient-held record for asylum seekers and refugees*. Downloadable files of patient-held records for asylum seekers and refugees, and their children, with patient instructions in various languages.
- *An introduction to the NHS for asylum seekers and refugees*. This covers issues such as the role of general practitioners, their function as gatekeepers to the health services, how to register and how to access emergency services. It is available for downloading in 40 languages.

Key points

- Applications for asylum in the UK and Europe are falling.
- Most applications are refused. While the number of appeals fell in 2005, almost one-fifth of applicants were found to have been wrongly refused asylum – 6080 people.
- Many asylum seekers are fleeing oppression and may have experienced traumatic events.
- Many asylum seekers are living below the poverty line and in poor accommodation which is likely to further impact on their health.
- A number of excellent specialist resources are available for health professionals working with asylum seekers and refugees.

References

Aspinall P (2006) *A Review of the Literature on the Health Beliefs, Health Status, Health Needs, and Use of Services in the Refugee and Asylum Seeker Population and of Appropriate Health and Social Care Interventions.* Health ASERT Programme, Wales

British Medical Association (2002) *Asylum seekers: Meeting their healthcare needs.*London, BMA Board of Science and Education

Buchanan S, Grillo B, Threadgold T (2003) What's the story? *Article 19*, London. www.article19.org

Burnett A, Fassil Y (2002) *Meeting the Health Needs of Refugee and Asylum Seekers in the UK: An Information and Resource Pack for Health Workers.* Department of Health, London

Burnett A, Peel M (2001) Health needs of asylum seekers and refugees. *British Medical Journal* **322:** 544–7

Fine B, Cheal C (2004) *Resource Pack to Help General Practitioners and Other Healthcare Professionals in the Work with Refugees and Asylum Seekers.* Lambeth PCT, London

Home Office (2006) Statistical Bulletin. http://www.homeoffice.gov.uk/rds/pdfs06/hosb1406.pdf

Home Office (2008) Asylum Statistics United Kingdom 2007. Home Office Statistical Bulletin. London, Home Office

McLeish J (2002) *Mothers in Exile: Maternity Experiences of Asylum Seekers in England.* Maternity Alliance, London

Refugee-Action (2006) *The Destitution Trap.* London, Refugee Action

Refugee Health Consortium (1998) *Promoting the Health of Refugees.* Refugee Health Consortium, London

Further resources

Information services

- NHS Evidence – ethnicity and health
  http://www.library.nhs.uk/ethnicity/
  Formerly one of the NHS Specialist Libraries for health this website provides electronic evidence relating to health care for minority ethnic groups in Britain.
- Race for Health Programme
  http://raceforhealth.org/whatsnew.php
  The Race for Health Programme provides a current awareness service on ethnicity and health.

Sources of statistical information

- Official Statistics
  http://www.statistics.gov.uk/
- BBC News Born Abroad
  http://news.bbc.co.uk/1/shared/spl/hi/uk/05/born_abroad/html/overview.stm

General organisations dealing with issues of racism, equality and minority ethnic groups

- Institute for Race Relations
  http://www.irr.org.uk/
- Equality and Human Rights Commission
  http://www.equalityhumanrights.com/
- Runnymede Trust
  http://www.runnymedetrust.org/

Health organisations

- Afiya Trust
  http://www.afiyatrust.org
- Department of Health
  http://www.dh.gov.uk
  Search 'ethnic + monitoring' for a practical guide to ethnic monitoring in the NHS and social care.
  Search 'race + equality' for Department of Health's Race Equality Scheme.

- Kings Fund, London
  http://www.kingsfund.org.uk
  The Kings Fund Library contains several reading lists on various aspects of ethnic minority health.

Organisations for refugees, asylum seekers and migrants

- Health For Asylum Seekers and Refugees Portal (HARP)
  http://www.harpweb.org.uk/index.php
- Joint Council for the Welfare of Immigrants
  http://www.jcwi.org.uk//
- Refugee Council
  http://www.refugeecouncil.org.uk/
- Medical Foundation for Care of Victims of Torture
  http://www.torturecare.org.uk/
- Information Centre about Asylum and Refugees in the UK (ICAR)
  http://www.icar.org.uk

Travellers

- Friends Families and Travellers
  http://www.gypsy-traveller.org/
- Travellers Aid Trust
  http://www.Travellersaidtrust.org
- Traveller Law Reform Project
  http://www.travellerslaw.org.uk
- Time Travellers
  http://www.time-travellers.org.uk

Language, translation and interpretation

- British Red Cross
  http://www.redcross.org.uk
  The British Red Cross has developed a phrasebook to help with basic understanding and communication in medical emergencies. The phrasebook contains 62 common medical questions and statements in 36 languages. Copies of the Emergency Multilingual Phrasebook are available from the website.
- Department of Health
- http://www.dh.gov.uk/
  Sections of the Red Cross Phrasebook in individual languages can also be downloaded as PDF versions from the Department of Health website

by searching for 'emergency + multilingual + phrasebook.

- Chartered Institute of Linguists 'Find an Interpreter' page
  http://www.iol.org.uk/linguist/default.asp?r=H8EMOEJBAG
- National Register of Public Service Interpreters
  http://www.nrpsi.co.uk/
- Language Line
  http://www.languageline.com/home.php
- National Literacy Trust
  http://www.literacytrust.org.uk/
- Association of Translation Companies
  http://www.atc.org.uk/

Mental health

- Chinese Mental Health Association
  http://www.cmha.org.uk
- Jewish Association for the Mentally Ill
  http://www.jamiuk.org/
- National Black and Minority Ethnic Mental Health Network
  http://www.bmementalhealth.org.uk/
- National Institute for Mental Health in England (NIMHE)
  http://nimhe.csip.org.uk
  NIMHE has a series of publications on best practice in working with several minority ethnic communities
- MIND (National Association for Mental Health)
  http://www.mind.org.uk
  MIND produce fact sheets on a range of minority ethnic groups

Substance use

- Harm Reduction Leaflet for Khat
  http://www.daap.org.uk/gifs/khat/KhatEnglishInside.gif

Food and drugs authorities

- Federation of Synagogues Kashrus (Kosher Certification)
  http://www.kfkosher.org/
- Halal Food Authority
  http://www.halalfoodauthority.co.uk/

Traditional healing systems

- Register of Chinese Herbal Medicine

http://www.rchm.co.uk
- London College of Traditional Acupuncture and Oriental Medicine
http://www.lcta.com

Sickle cell and thalassaemia

- Accessible Publishing of Genetic Information. [APoGI Project]
http://www.chime.ucl.ac.uk/APoGI/
- NHS Sickle Cell and Thalassaemia Screening Programme
http://sct.screening.nhs.uk/
- Sickle Cell Society.
http://www.sicklecellsociety.org/
- UK Thalassaemia Society
http://www.ukts.org/

Miscellaneous

- Inter-faith Network for the UK
http://www.interfaith.org.uk/
- Ethnicity Online Cultural Awareness in Health Care
http://www.ethnicityonline.net/
- An example of a fatwa bank
http://www.islamonline.net/
- Religious calendars
http://www.multiculturalcalendar.com/index.php
- Channel 4: Origination: The Rich Mix of British Culture and History
http://www.channel4.com/culture/microsites/O/origination/
- Race for Health
http://www.raceforhealth.org/news_detail.php?id=64
This website contains a basic guide to infertility and its treatment in English, Urdu, Bengali, Punjabi, Gujarati.
- The National Learning Disability and Ethnicity Network
http://www.lden.org.uk/

Around the world

The following sites provide an overview of different countries, their politics, and the range of ethnic groups in that country:
- BBC News Country Profiles
http://news.bbc.co.uk/1/hi/country_profiles/default.stm
- Oxfam
http://www.oxfam.org

Oxfam maintains a briefing on many countries from whom the UK has, and may in the future have, refugees or migrants.

- New Internationalist
  http://www.newint.org/
  This magazine has as back catalogue of country profiles, although some of these may be dated.
- The US Central Intelligence Agency
  http://www.cia.gov/cia/publications/factbook
- Index Mundi (detailed country profiles compiled from multiple sources)
  http://www.indexmundi.com/

Research centres

- Centre for Ethnicity and Health, Institute for Philosophy, Diversity and Mental Health, University of Central Lancashire
  http://www.uclan.ac.uk
- Research Centre for Transcultural Studies in Health, Middlesex University
  http://www.mdx.ac.uk/www/rctsh/
- Mary Seacole Research Centre, De Montfort University, Leicester
  http://www.dmu.ac.uk/msrc
- Mary Seacole Centre for Nursing Practice, Thames Valley University
  http://www.maryseacole.com
- PRIAE - Policy Research Institute on Ageing and Ethnicity
  http://www.priae.org
  This independent research group specialises in issues associated with age, including palliative care and research into the treatment of older people across Europe.
- North East London Consortium for Research and Development (NELCRAD)
  http://www.nelcrad.nhs.uk
- Unit for the Social Study of Thalassaemia and Sickle Cell, De Montfort University
  http://www.tascunit.com

Mailing lists

- JISCmail
  http://www.jiscmail.ac.uk/
  Visit this website to subscribe to very helpful lists on minority ethnic health and ethnicity and reproduction.
- Research Centre for Transcultural Studies in Health
  http://www.mdx.ac.uk/www/rctsh

Research Centre for Transcultural Studies in Health at Middlesex University also operates a mailing list.

- MIGHEALTHNET
  http://mighealth.net/index/Main_Page
  This website has a European perspective on migration and health.

Index